HOW TO
CHOOSE A
CAREER

HOW TO CHOOSE A CAREER

FOURTH EDITION

VIVIEN DONALD

KOGAN
PAGE

First published in 1986
Second edition 1989
Third edition 1993
Fourth edition 1996

Kogan Page Limited
120 Pentonville Road
London N1 9JN

© Vivien Donald 1986, 1989, 1993, 1996

British Library Cataloguing in Publication Data

A CIP record for this book is available from the British Library.

ISBN 0 7494 1934 2

Typeset by DP Photosetting, Aylesbury, Bucks
Printed and bound in Great Britain by
Clays Ltd, St Ives plc

Contents

squeamish? 84; Could you cope with shift work or
unsocial hours? 84; Health and physique 85; Could you
cope with a long period of study? 86

Full-time education 95; Courses in Art and Design 100;
Courses in Teacher Training 101; City and Guilds 101;
Certificate of Pre-vocational Education 101; National
Vocational Qualifications (NVQs) 101; General
National Vocational Qualifications (GNVQs) 102;
Royal Society of Arts (RSA) 103; Courses in Land-
based Industries 103; Training for Work 103; Modern
Apprenticeships 103; Youth Training 104; Youth
Credits 104; Timing of applications 105; If you fail to
get a college place 107

Grants 108; Loans 110; Sponsorships 111

Introduction

When people are in their early teens, with the 'options evening' at school imminent, their thoughts of a career are liable still to be wildly optimistic: a fighter pilot, pop star, famous model – famous anything! So they select their options from the subjects that they are good at, their parents and teachers are pleased, and they hope that those subjects will be the ones to launch them on the road to success.

That choice may well turn out to be right, and lead to a good career; but it is very easy at this stage to drop subjects that are needed for specific careers – and to make the discovery too late. That is why it helps to have some kind of career aim in view as early as possible, to make subject choices easier and to give you a goal to work towards. While it is true that it does not always take academic brilliance to be successful, rich and famous, it does take application; and increasingly these days, the high-flyers are those who have had good basic training of some kind. There may be a large number of other enthusiasts chasing after the college course or company training scheme place that you have set your heart on, so the more useful GCSEs and A level or Higher subjects that you have, the better.

The good news is that there is a greater diversity of higher education courses than ever before, but you need to choose your course with care, so that your time at college is not wasted. The number of unskilled jobs has dropped, and it is important to aim for the right qualifications to land a good skilled job. There are plenty of opportunities for those who look in the right places; the expanding industry of information technology, for instance, is short of software staff with expertise in analysis, design and programming. The leisure and tourism industry is getting bigger, too, all part of the general growth in service industries.

In many industries, the 'job for life' pattern is becoming outdated, and there is a growing trend for people to work on short-term temporary contracts, hiring out their knowledge, rather than their time. In this type of environment they need to build up their skills so that eventually they have a 'portfolio of skills' to offer.

Recognising your own skills will help in making the choice of which direction to take. Decide which are the ones that will be of most value and are worth developing through courses and training. It may be that your ambition to become a doctor, for instance, goes out of the window, but that you have just the qualities needed in another career allied to medicine.

You don't always need professional qualifications to end up in an interesting job: hard work, flair and just being in the right place at the right time can get you there as well (an advantage of 'temping' work). But you can't rely on such attributes alone; a professional qualification, a degree that is attractive to employers or the right technical training can give you a better chance in the job market.

Of course, there are many hundreds of different types of job and career; if you have no idea at all of what you want to do, choosing from among so many is a confusing business. Between accountant and actuary at the beginning of the careers list, and zoo vet at the end, there are possibilities of all kinds. However, while there are hundreds of accountants, working in every kind of industry and situation, there are relatively few actuaries (who work with statistics and the theory of mathematical probability, usually in insurance companies), and even fewer zoo vets. So it makes sense to aim for qualifications and a career where you will be in demand, rather than find yourself – at the end of perhaps a great deal of work – in a market where prospects are shrinking rather than expanding.

In choosing a career you will also want to find something that suits your own particular talents (academic or otherwise), your likes and dislikes, and your assessment of your personality and capabilities. Parents naturally expect great things of their offspring, but only you yourself know what you would really be happiest doing.

Part 1

1. Good Prospects

From what you have learned at school and seen on television, you will know that manufacturing industries producing goods such as ships and textiles are less active in Britain than they once were, but that exciting new things are happening in electronics and information technology; and service industries, such as catering, leisure and tourism are now major employers.

To help you get an idea of where your interests and talents might fit and be in demand in the future, the first half of this book gives a very brief picture of a selection of organisations, industries and professions and some of the possible kinds of career within them. Some of the industries, such as construction (the building of everything from houses and roads, to airports) have been around for a very long time; others are more recent, expanding, and constantly developing new technology.

INFORMATION TECHNOLOGY

Information technology has come a long way since Alexander Graham Bell invented the telephone 120 years ago but without it there would be no telecommunications revolution, no optical fibre superhighways and no Internet. Perhaps the telephone really is 'the world's most important patent', as it was once described. Whatever the case, we can be sure that Mr Bell would be amazed by the way we communicate today.

Virtual reality software and multimedia programmes have created a new world where the user can participate directly in three-dimensional environments. Architects, for example, can show potential customers what it would be like to walk through rooms not yet built. Virtual reality can also be used in conjunction with robotics to carry out repairs in environments that are too dangerous for humans.

Holography (the production of three-dimensional images using lasers) is used by pilots and pop stars alike to enhance their performance. Now it is expected to transform the storage of information. Data storage is an information technology industry and depends heavily on the use of computers.

Computers are an integral part of telecommunications; they are used, for instance, in weather forecasting and ship navigation to interpret signals received from satellites. They are also, of course, used extensively in the business world (mainframe computers, desk-top terminals and microcomputers) and there are plenty of personal computers to be found in the home, too, especially as more work is done by consultants and freelance workers from home. In the manufacturing process, robots, the responsibility of mechanical engineers, are used to carry out the minute-scale, delicate tasks that are too intricate for relatively ham-fisted people to do.

The companies involved in communications and computers need to concentrate assiduously on research, in order to keep ahead of worldwide competition. Many companies in fact incorporate components into their equipment that are made abroad. But research by electronics engineers and laboratory technicians is going on all the time, finding new and better ways of sending and storing information and improving existing methods, so those who want to acquire a skill that is certain to be in demand should work at their maths and physics and take them at A level.

Chemists, materials scientists and physicists are always in demand, as they are needed to develop new integrated circuit products and superconductors like Pentium, which increase the speed at which information travels.

In conjunction with the manufacture of the 'hardware', the computers themselves, is the booming production of software – the disks or tapes containing computer programs. Anyone who has a computer at home or who has done computer studies at school will know that a computer is able to do very complex calculations very quickly indeed, that it can store and memorise information fed into it, process the information and display it.

In the business world, computers have taken on an enormous amount of tedious and boring work. They are used for stock control, for accounting systems, to help in forward planning, to send out mailing lists, and to help with planning timetables like the ones used for schools, railways or airlines. They can calculate wages, print out pay slips and keep records, make hotel reservations and, with their capacity for displaying three-dimensional objects through CAD (computer-aided design), help in engineering design and the creation of the graphics that you see on television. Typists are saved work by the word processors that can print out material stored in memory banks, and by fax machines that send a copy of a document along phone lines to be printed out instantly by a similar machine at the other end of the line – which may be on the opposite side of the world.

So the use of information technology can obviously save a great deal of time and money, and has also led to the development of new skills and jobs that were unheard of not many years ago.

Before computers can be used effectively in a business context, they have to be programmed to produce maximum savings in costs. The shopkeeper or person running a small business would probably be able to do this for themselves, but large businesses would need a team of experts to define exactly what tasks the computer, or computers, should perform and then to prepare the necessary programs. On some projects this could take years, and involve a large number of people. Those who work out the tasks the computers must do are called systems analysts: next the systems designers take over and work out how the computers should be programmed to do the tasks identified by the systems analysts; computer programmers then 'translate' the designers' instructions into the language used by the computers and write out a program; and finally, the computers are used by computer operators, who are trained to feed information into the machine via the keyboard or other input device and to use the disks or tapes on which information is stored.

Many jobs in computing, such as that of systems analyst, are highly skilled and can be well paid. Lower down the line, VDU operators start at around £8500 per annum, and programmers at £13,800 upwards (1995 figures). Although the highest salary for a graduate trainee is £20,000, the average is more likely to be around £15,000. Because it is a new science, with no long-term tradition of male employment, it is work in which women can specialise and do well. An advantage of computer programming as a career is that it is one of the jobs that can often be done at home by those who are also bringing up a family or who are disabled.

After the actual manufacturing process, it is the marketing teams who have to go out and sell both the hardware and software to users (against stiff competition) and, once the computers are in position, highly trained maintenance engineers (who are often electrical or mechanical engineering graduates with university training) are needed to service them.

Because information technology is expanding and changing all

13

the time, careers and specialisations within the industry are also changing, and sometimes overlapping with other specialisations. Expertise in working with computers is demanded by a wide variety of users, including government departments and the armed services, commercial businesses, research centres, local authorities, hospitals and many more. It can often turn out to be an advantage to have done a computer studies or science course at school or college, though employers are interested in applicants with a wide variety of qualifications. There is expected to be an increased demand for IT staff, especially analyst/programmers and network/data communications staff.

ELECTRONICS INDUSTRY

Like information technology, electronics is based on innovative new skills and sciences and it is another area in which highly skilled and qualified staff are in demand – especially, of course, electronics engineers.

Very often equipment designed and developed by electronics engineers for military use (a lot of it for sale to countries overseas) is then adapted for civilian purposes. End-products include systems used for monitoring under-water conditions around oil rigs, infra-red cameras to help firemen 'see' through smoke, remotely controlled vehicles, cellular phones, and airborne surveillance systems which can pinpoint vessels in trouble at sea. Companies specialising in electronics are also involved in space technology: providing communications packages and computer link-ups for satellites used for meteorological purposes and for surveillance.

Although a large number of electronics engineers work for companies which develop technology for defence, such as GEC-Marconi, Britain's largest engineering business, the peace initiative has come at a time when interest in civilian communication technologies has mushroomed, the result of which has been to shift slightly the pace and direction of research.

Because information technology requires constant innovation electronics companies have to keep ahead of the game by designing and developing new products that increase the speed at which information data can be sent, retrieved or exchanged. These include new integrated circuits in telecommunications equipment, new and more advanced control systems for use in avionics and for the monitoring of information, household products like videos and multimedia game units, process controls for manufacturing, tools for environmental monitoring and surgical equipment used in medicine.

Apart from electronics engineers, electronics companies are also keen to recruit systems designers and software engineers and a certain number of mechanical engineers. In companies of this kind it is the professionals, those who hold degrees, who have the chance to become involved in running the business and in contributing ideas. Many of the people joining them each year will have electronic or electrical engineering degrees, or sometimes engineering with electronics options. Those interested in the software side can be from computer science courses, physical science, applied mathematics, electronics and also from mechanical engineering. There is a shortage in this field that is likely to remain for some time, and so a degree course virtually guarantees a job.

It is not too soon to start thinking of studying for this type of degree as early as the age of 11 or 12, because it is important to continue with maths and physics – girls, too! Engineering is a profession which needs more women. The Engineering Council, the Engineering Training Council (EnTra) and the Institute of Electronics and Electrical Incorporated Engineers all produce publications and videos designed specifically for girls thinking of a career in engineering.

Although many professional engineers join a company after they have taken a degree, there is a good alternative. The modern apprenticeship in engineering manufacture is designed for people with good GCSE grades in maths, English and science subjects. Developed by EnTra in association with local Training and Enterprise Centres, or LECs in Scotland, the modern apprentice receives a high standard of training, both in the workplace and at college. Modern apprentices are employed for the duration of the apprenticeship and receive a wage agreed between the individual and the employer. They then follow an individual training plan, agreed at the start, which sets out exactly what is to be achieved, usually a National Vocational Qualification up to level 4. If you are 18 or 19 and have studied for A levels, a BTEC qualification or a General National Vocational Qualification, you may be able to start an 'accelerated' modern apprenticeship. For more details contact EnTra on Freephone 0800 282167. Alternatively, get in touch with one of the major companies or your local TEC or LEC.

GEC-Marconi are one of the major companies involved in sponsoring students for courses in electrical/electronic engineering, as well as other subjects including physics, engineering, computer science, mathematics and business subjects. The four-, five- and six-year sandwich courses combine planned work experience with the company with a degree course at a college; the different companies within GEC-Marconi have their own requirements and the courses are often taken at specified universities. This gives the best of both worlds: because the student's holiday is used for training within the company, by the end of the degree course he or she knows both the academic aspects of the subject and its practical applications, as well as the future aims and prospects for the industry.

Under this scheme people doing the course become virtual employees of the company at A level, and the final course project leads straight into a job. Sponsored students fulfilling the required standards are not normally turned down for a job as a lot of money has been invested in them – the bursary, plus payments to them, and administration overheads. Some companies also run technician engineer schemes for A level students who can then study for an HND (Higher National Diploma).

A number of other companies offer sponsorship schemes similar to GEC-Marconi and a complete list is available from the Schools Liaison Service of the Institution of Mechanical Engineers (for address see page 119); but to give you a few examples they include Ove Arup and Partners, the BBC, the Army, Ford Motor Company and Midlands Electricity.

Applications for university sponsorships are high; perhaps 2500 applicants each year for 50 places. The companies look for high grades and people with the sort of personality that makes them likely to do well: those who can motivate others and demonstrate leadership potential – ultimately, sponsored students are likely to go through into management, and maybe even senior management.

Some people find they are very much better suited to going into industry at GCSE level if they enjoy technical work and being with people, and prefer a day-release course and the firm's own training. While studying at college can seem to some people like working in a vacuum, without any practical idea of what the work is for, in industry there is more contact with a project: students can be walked to the end of the production line and shown the end result.

Other possible career openings within electrical companies are: draughtsman, or more commonly, technician, working in large drawing offices, with possible scope for promotion to management; materials scientist, involved with ceramics (for use in electrical and electronic components, and in diesel and jet engines), glasses, polymers and other materials; mathematician; mechanical engineer; physicist; and some chemical engineers. People with non-technical degrees are rarely taken on, except in personnel and other management departments.

All the engineering institutions produce books, pamphlets, videos and cassettes offering advice and information on training, education and career opportunities. It is well worth contacting some of the organisations listed on pages 117–21. Average starting salary for electronics engineers in 1995 was £14,500.

PHARMACEUTICALS

The emphasis on recruiting in the large pharmaceutical companies is different. For, although the pharmaceuticals industry is an important one, the success of individual companies depends on how well they hold their position in the market against their competitors. Getting out and selling their products is vital in overseas markets as well as at home. This means that highly qualified people may be employed in the marketing department of a company, and their qualifications may not necessarily be science-based.

The R & D (research and development) department is concerned with devising new products that will appeal to buyers, and with improving existing ones. The chemicals that they work with and research into are not only the drugs needed by human and veterinary medicine, which are produced by the pharmaceutical companies: other interests include man-made fibres like nylon and polyester, used for clothing and furnishings; tyres for motor vehicles; plastic packaging; and dyes. Aware that electronics is a fast-developing field, some of the research is into possible uses for chemical products within the electronics industry; for instance, materials used in the production of the silicon chip; dyestuffs for liquid crystal displays; the plastics used in electronic components; audio, video and computer tapes; and computer disks. Investigations are also going on to see if it is possible to replace the optical fibres used in telecommunications with polymers.

As plastics are basically forms of solidified oil, the plastics companies have interests in the North Sea and other oilfields throughout the world. However, the R & D scientists are also trying to develop new materials that can replace some of the plastics with others that are not reliant on oil.

The chemicals industry also covers agricultural applications. Chemicals are used to kill weeds and fungi that cut down crop yields, to get rid of pests such as flies, aphids and rodents, and to boost harvests.

The main areas of R & D are in biology and biotechnology, in new materials, and in new uses for products. There is likely to be a more biologically-based rather than an oil-based chemicals industry in the future, as the world's supply of oil diminishes. Biotechnology, a multi-disciplinary science, will then be applied to the problems of increasing the world's food supply, satisfying energy needs, and to pollution and health considerations. Biodegradable plastics, based on vegetable products, are vital for environmental protection. Even computers could go biological!

Although employment is not guaranteed for all those with degrees in biological sciences, there will be some very interesting research work around for those who do end up in commercial research laboratories. Subjects could include monoclonal anti-bodies, vaccines, hormones, enzymes, other proteins and gene therapy for genetic diseases, plant growth hormones and micro-bial pesticides. If you are a dedicated scientist, you could eventually find yourself doing some fascinating work along these lines.

Suitable science-based degrees for R & D work may be in such subjects as chemistry, physics, organic chemistry, biochemistry, materials science, metallurgy, physical and synthetic polymer chemistry, colloid chemistry, or maths. R & D staff may move on to work in other fields within a company, such as production and sales, and through to senior management.

A science degree can also lead to a job in the marketing department, where the staff are normally highly qualified. Marketing may involve identifying a new use for a chemical that has been developed for something else, or that is a by-product of another process. Successful marketing means finding new markets which may involve spending a lot of time out of the country; a language degree is therefore a good non-technical qualification. Other acceptable degrees for this type of work could include economics, business studies, or even geography, but the most important asset is having the right personality – with drive, good business judgement, resilience, stamina and the ability to get on well with people.

As manufacturers, the chemical companies employ chemical

and process engineers (who design the plant used to make the products), production engineers and managers (in charge of production processes), and mechanical and electrical engineers. Some of the plant may be sited overseas, and expert engineering staff could have the opportunity for spells of work abroad.

Like the electronics companies, the chemicals and drugs companies offer sponsorship to university students, although not on the same scale.

There are also large numbers of people employed as laboratory assistants and environmental research assistants, who are taken on at GCSE level and A level stage and given training based on day release (though often only applicants who live locally are considered). There are also schemes for engineering (design and project work) and technical apprenticeships for GCSE level students (again, applicants should live locally).

Those who intend to study science at university, or who are already doing so, may be able to take advantage of the chance that chemicals and drugs companies offer to work as laboratory assistants in the year before going to university and during the vacations. But demand for these places is high and numbers are limited, so it is a good idea to ask the course tutor at the university for the names of companies that have established links with the university and are therefore more likely to offer a place. Students should expect to spend at least six months, and preferably nine, with the company.

It should be said that although the chemicals and drugs businesses form a large industry, science graduates do not always find themselves working in purely scientific jobs. However, their skills can be used in other ways – not only in the marketing and R & D departments mentioned, but also in related fields, such as computing, accounting, banking, nuclear power, pollution control and various manufacturing industries. The average starting salary for graduate chemical engineers is £15,000.

MULTINATIONALS

Large multinational companies with interests that range from ice cream to shampoos are interested in biotechnology too, and also employ scientists in their research laboratories. A large organisation such as Unilever employs thousands of people at all levels in countries throughout the world.

If you go into a large supermarket, you will see that many of the goods on sale there are produced by one company, although

19

under different brand names. Sausages and soaps, frozen meals and fabric conditioners, teas and toothpaste may all be the products of one organisation. The growth in popularity of ready-prepared foods and household products – and even men's toiletries – has helped these businesses, and their interests cover wide areas. They may have their own packaging companies and deal with their own transport – involving warehousing, distribution to shops and stores, maybe coastal shipping and freight forwarding for carrying both raw materials and end-products.

Although these large organisations have subsidiaries and even plantations scattered throughout the world, these will be employing nationals of the countries themselves, so there is not necessarily the chance to work abroad except in the short term, when experts may be sent to give advice on management, finance, engineering, research or marketing, or trainees in management may be sent to broaden their experience.

In the research laboratories scientists work in a variety of disciplines but with an emphasis on biological sciences, from microbial fermentation to genetic engineering and from immunology to physics (one interesting project has been the cloning of oil palms whose products are used in margarine and cooking oils; work is now in progress on the cloning of coconut palms). Toxicology and bacteriology are important subjects, too, because products that go on to the market must have been proved to be safe.

The bulk of the staff within an organisation of this kind work in management, and training may be at the company's own training colleges, or on-the-job training combined with courses at business schools and universities. Computers are now indispensable for design engineering, planning, communications, stock control and so forth, and their use calls for the skills of systems analysts, data processors and programmers. Other specialists employed include engineers of many disciplines, particularly chemical, mechanical, production (manufacturing, electrical/electronic and control engineers), as well as structural engineers (with the responsibility of maintaining office and factory buildings) and other maintenance staff.

CONSTRUCTION INDUSTRY

Whereas information technology and electronics firms are reaping the benefits of a buoyant market, the construction industry is only now beginning to pick up after the recession.

20

However, there is always work to be done and new and challenging projects to be involved with.

Forty per cent of all building work is repair and maintenance. The rest includes new projects like proposed Channel Tunnel rail links, the new River Severn crossing, city shopping centres, housing, power stations and so on. In essence the construction industry provides the essential infrastructure for modern living; without it there would be no hospitals, schools, roads, railways, sports centres or shops.

Construction activity follows the growth area of business, and workers must be prepared to be flexible and often to travel. British construction companies often work on projects abroad and individuals will sometimes need to head to where their services are in demand. Although prospects for builders in Britain are better than they were, many British builders temporarily migrate to countries where demand for builders exceeds supply, for example Germany.

Specific careers within the building industry are those of civil, structural and building engineering and building services. Civil engineering means, roughly speaking, construction at or below ground level: roads, bridges, tunnels, and the foundations of buildings. Civil engineers work closely with architects to produce detailed structural designs of building projects. They then supervise the construction and are responsible for the management of materials and labour on site, ensuring building work happens on time and within budgetary constraints. They are employed by private companies, local authorities and government departments like the Highways Agency.

Structural engineers make sure designs are safe. They are employed by manufacturers of structures who have to be sure that their suspension bridge doesn't buckle in the first gale or that their oil platform or boat won't sink in a storm.

Building and building services engineers design, construct and maintain buildings. They have an in-depth knowledge of statutory regulations and the law and are responsible for the day-to-day practicalities of projects, such as which building material should be used. Other professionals include quantity surveyors and architects who normally work independently of the construction companies, in consultancy partnerships. Major construction companies may also employ geotechnical, mechanical, electrical and chemical engineers, and materials scientists. Sponsorships and work experience are offered to students studying for degrees that include quantity surveying, civil engineering, building and

21

building services engineering. Those who are offered a place with the company once they have gained their degree are then given further training which leads to professional qualifications.

Technicians in building and civil engineering are taken on by large building contractors after they have taken their GCSE or A levels and trained on day-release courses – either a BTEC or building course. In a large company, most will remain at a fairly junior level, although some may reach middle management and even become project or contract managers (arranging the details of contract work); alternatively, a very small minority may continue training and reach professional status, but this is fairly rare. It is also possible to complete vocational training through a modern apprenticeship, as described in the section on electronic engineering. This could lead to an NVQ or SVQ in construction and engineering.

Many of these people will need to be able to work with computers, widely used in the building industry to help with the sophisticated planning that goes into a large project.

Part of that planning, of course, involves the interior of the building, as well as the outside, and here another group of professionals is employed in the design, construction and maintenance. These are the building services (or environmental) engineers, who are responsible for the planning of heating and ventilation, lifts, lighting and communication systems, water supply and so on; working with them are the mechanical and electrical engineers who are responsible not only for the installation of the necessary equipment, but for its future maintenance, long after the builders have departed.

Those wanting to know more about careers in construction should contact the Institution of Civil Engineers, the Institution of Structural Engineers, the Association of Building Engineers, the Construction Industry Training Board and the Chartered Institute of Building.

SERVICE INDUSTRIES

As opposed to the manufacturing industries that make goods such as cars and washing machines, service industries include banking and insurance, leisure and entertainment and the more personal types of work like hairdressing and nursing. It is with the service industries that the opportunities for many people now choosing a career will lie in the future.

LEISURE AND ENTERTAINMENT

For a variety of reasons, people have more leisure time nowadays to take part in sports, watch television, read magazines, or go on family outings. Cheap package holidays mean they are more likely to go away for a fortnight of Mediterranean sun or winter skiing. Sightseeing tourists come to Britain, too, to visit stately homes, Shakespeare country, theatres and museums – and to go shopping in Oxford Street.

This is good business for civil aviation and its related activities. A new super-terminal, with new road links and new rail station, is planned for Heathrow airport. It is due to open in 2002, and to be completed by 2016, ready to cope with twice as many passengers as now, both business and tourist – around 80 million annually. A new terminal at Stansted airport has already been completed.

Eventually there could be as many as 15 million passengers going through Stansted in one year, with around 15,000 people employed there, including airport and airline management, flight deck crews, air traffic controllers, customs and immigration officers, security officers, freight-handling companies, aircraft maintenance staff, craftsmen, clerical staff, cabin crews, loaders, porters, caterers and cleaners, and all the people employed in the shops, cafés and restaurants that will rent space within the terminal buildings.

In the area surrounding the airport, too, there will be indirect employment through hotels and shops and the building of new houses for people working at the airport.

Tourism provides a large number of jobs, though many of them need no special skills and may be seasonal and not very well paid. These include staff in travel agencies, airlines, car hire firms, tour guides, leisure park and sports ground attendants, and management staff in all these occupations.

A large slice of the tourism cake is taken up with all kinds of accommodation, from bed-and-breakfast to huge hotels. Again, many of these jobs are unskilled; the better paid are in management. Both hotel management and catering are areas in which you can study for qualifications and work your way up the promotional ladder. These days, many of the good management jobs are taken by graduates, who may already have had training in hotel management. Management staff also hold BTEC or SCOTVEC qualifications or NVQ/SVQs. There are many opportunities in catering, because it covers not only hotels, restaurants and fast-food bars used by private customers, but also the canteens provided by most large companies for their staff, which are often run by catering agencies.

The other side of the leisure industry is that of entertainment: theatres, cinemas, television, magazines and newspapers. Television is an expanding area at the moment, with four channels demanding material to fill air time, a fifth in prospect, day-long transmissions the aim of the major channels, cable and satellite television, and the imminent start of digital television.

This activity does not guarantee employment for all aspiring actresses and actors, writers, producers and presenters. Acting, we are continually told, is a hazardous and overcrowded profession where very few make a good living or become famous. Even for those who have qualified, it can also be very difficult to find backstage work.

Behind the microphones and cameras of radio and television are production teams, administration and secretarial staff, journalists and presenters. Producers and their assistants and members of the journalistic team are expected to hold a degree; competition for jobs is fierce. Secretarial and administrative staff very rarely get the chance to transfer to the production or presentation side, so there is little point in hoping to get into radio or television in that way.

Both the BBC and independent television companies have training schemes for their staff. Local radio provides a good training ground for many production and journalistic staff. Engineers, who work on sound and lighting, are recruited for training with a degree in electrical, electronic or communication engineering. Engineering assistants and trainee studio managers may be recruited with GCSEs or equivalent in English, maths and physics.

Independent of the work done by the main television companies is the work done by an increasing number of production companies who provide programmes for television stations. They also produce advertising films used on commercial television and video for documentaries, pop record promotions and educational purposes.

A great deal of radio time is filled, as you know, with pop music, which is a thriving business. There are many hopefuls who see themselves as another Madonna or Michael Jackson, or who hope to make it to the top of the charts as one of a group. It's an uncertain game, though, and the best advice is: have a go, by all means, but acquire fail-safe qualifications at the same time.

Those who are most certain of making money in the pop world are the retailers and promoters.

The written word, as opposed to the sung or spoken word, is a flourishing aspect of entertainment at the moment: think of all the magazines on the bookstalls, the free papers, local papers and business-to-business magazines. Linked to these are the related fields of advertising and publicity. National newspaper staff are now normally taken on as graduates, with local newspaper experience, and there is a training programme that both reporters and press photographers must follow. In the area of magazine journalism, advertising and publicity, a degree may be an advantage, but it is possible to work your way up from the bottom, even from a secretarial post.

The whole leisure, catering and entertainment industry is constantly developing, reflecting changing social moods and economic situations. It is an industry in which the entrepreneur can spot an opportunity to build up a thriving business, and where it is possible to move easily from one type of work to another.

OTHER PEOPLE'S MONEY

The financial world may not seem very close to the entertainment business, and the meteoric rise (and fall) of stars, but there are a few hyperactive young men (and women!) in the Stock Exchange who earn sums as City analysts that many a pop star would envy – though normally they 'burn out' by the time they are aged 30, and turn to some other form of financial work.

The financial services provided by people on the Stock Exchange, and in banking and insurance and other business services, are extremely valuable, not only to private individuals and companies within Britain, but to countries overseas as well. Financial services are a significant part of Britain's 'invisible earnings' – money earned from the export of services as opposed to actual products.

Insurers cover houses and cars, but also space satellites, yachts, tankers (which might be carrying dangerous cargoes), pipelines and construction projects in the Middle East and Africa.

In fact, insurers will cover practically anything, from a famous actress's legs to the Telecom Tower, plus endowment policies and life assurance (life insurance is known as assurance in the trade). Handling pensions and the investment of funds are also part of an insurance company's business. Many jobs in insurance involve contact with the public, so it helps to be able to get on well with people. Young people who are not highly qualified but have the right temperament can train on the job after they have taken GCSEs and can do very well. Many also go into insurance with A levels or degrees, but graduates tend to find management roles rather than work in selling. Qualifications and courses are organised by the Chartered Insurance Institute.

The main areas of work are: selling (very important), insurance broking (matching up insurance to clients' needs), claims work, investment management, computer management, surveying (a qualified surveyor assesses damage and prepares a report for the claims staff), actuarial work (evaluating statistics and assessing life assurance) and underwriting (deciding whether it is worth taking on each risk, and how much the premium should be).

The retail (as opposed to corporate) arm of banking is another business in which personal skills have become much more important as the banks compete against the building societies, insurance companies and even large retailers such as Marks & Spencer. It is essential that the staff in the high street branch have the right type of personality; building up a rapport with customers is an essential part of the service. Behind the scenes staff in the central processing unit handle the cheques, banker's orders, statements and so on. Here they are mainly clerical, and as numbers of bank staff have decreased, may be employed on short-term contracts when the volume of work demands it.

There is less moving around now among departments – and around the country – in retail banking, although those marked out for top management need to get experience in different areas. Staff enter banks at different levels: school or college leavers may be taken on as clerical assistants; a qualification such as a BTEC ND in Business and Finance starts you off at a higher grade and graduates enter a management scheme with an induction course. The degree can be in any subject. Those going into management often need to become very involved with the local community, both on a private and business level. A branch manager will help small businesses with loans and advice, and must be able to assess profitability. Another trend among bank staff is specialisation in areas such as insurance, investment and fund management.

The type of fund management handled by banks on behalf of their customers is in low-risk areas. There are also businesses that specialise in handling higher risk funds on behalf of large companies, pension funds, charities and wealthy people, and for governments and their central banks. Fund management is a growing industry and top fund managers (usually based in London and usually with degrees in economics) can earn very high commissions on profitable investments.

London is a centre for international banking. Most banks have international divisions dealing with countries, customers and currencies all over the world. They give advice on trading conditions abroad, deal in foreign stocks and shares and handle shipping documents. Although staff do not often get the chance to travel abroad themselves, they deal with people overseas all the time, and so foreign languages would be useful qualifications.

Another banking activity based in the City is merchant banking, which concentrates on giving financial backing and advice to businesses, including advising companies both in Britain and abroad on investments, takeovers and mergers. Merchant banks also handle pension funds and the issuing of shares, and are involved in bullion (gold) dealing, shipping insurance broking and commodity trading. Some of these activities overlap with other business – insurance broking, for example. The London Investment Banking Association provides a list of those banks which recruit graduates.

Commodity dealing is a fascinating business that is also firmly fixed in London. Deals are handled between foreign countries in goods that may never land in Britain (although once they would have done). These goods include barley and wheat, cocoa, coffee, rubber and sugar (the 'soft' commodities) and aluminium, copper, lead, nickel, silver, tin and zinc. Goods are also traded at auction and in sale rooms: goods that must be inspected, such as tea and furs, are sold at auctions while others, such as fibres, gums, nuts, herbs and spices are sold in sale rooms. Commodity markets often trade in 'futures' – buying and selling at prices fixed for up to nine months ahead. Buying of this kind may be in gas-oil or even potatoes, and sudden changes in factors such as the price of oil or the weather in Brazil (where coffee is grown) can lead to large profits – or losses.

Apart from financial services, there are various other types of business service including advertising and public relations (liaison with the press and public to promote a company's interests), computer software, management consultancy, employment agencies, market research, the running of exhibition and conference centres, office cleaning, land and estate companies, estate agencies, copying of documents and translation. These are areas of work where skill and talent, rather than specific professional qualifications, can be the passport to an interesting career.

27

PERSONAL SERVICE

Personal services are those given on a direct personal basis, such as hairdressing, and health and beauty therapy. Their growth is partly the result of people having more leisure and time to indulge themselves, and partly because more people are living longer and need to be cared for.

Services for old people include medical care, and there will be an increasing need for nurses and doctors specialising in geriatric medicine, and for chiropodists, of whom there is already a shortage. Other types of service geared to the needs of the elderly are holidays and entertainments, clothing, sheltered housing and retirement homes, and welfare work.

Personal services also include children's nannies (who often care for children while both parents are out at work), cleaning, gardening and maintenance work. Many of the jobs are unskilled, others require training. With the growth in the need for personal services, they can offer the chance of success for those who enjoy working with people. Qualifications range from NVQ Level 1 to degree level.

RETAILING

Although clothes shops, stationers and greengrocers are inclined to appear and disappear with sometimes bewildering rapidity along the high street, the supermarkets, hypermarkets and chain stores are more firmly entrenched. They pay very strict attention to the profit they will make on the goods they sell. Managers and staff must be well trained.

Management training schemes take on people with GCSE grade C or above in maths and English, and A level/Higher or BTEC/SCOTVEC qualifications, but many of these places are being competed for by graduates. The large retailing chains have graduate entry schemes in management and in buying, marketing and merchandising. Graduate training scheme entrants will have degrees in any discipline or HND subjects but there are now many degree courses in retail management. At A level entry, some experience in a relevant field, including management of people, is a useful extra qualification – this could be as school prefect or team captain. Those whose initial applications look good then go through a rigorous process of interviews.

Survivors of the interviews then take part in training schemes, learning eventually about the complicated tasks of stock control, buying and selling, promotions, storage, staff relations and so on. Trainees specialise in either commercial, administration, or personnel management. Some people drop out during the training period, disillusioned by the very high standards expected, but as it can cost over £10,000 to train a management recruit for a year, the employers naturally try to take on people who they think will stick at the training – even so, they may lose trainees during the first year. Starting salaries for school-leavers are around £10,500, for graduates £14,000 (1995).

Apart from the chance of earning high salaries for those who get to the top management positions, working for one of the large chains does mean being provided with benefits such as staff discounts on goods, medical treatment, sickness benefits, pension schemes, subsidised meals, sports and social facilities, personal insurance – even, perhaps, free hairdressing. It also, of course, means very hard work and unsocial hours, though many large firms work a rota so that not all weekends are spent at the store.

Retailing, as you will have guessed, is another area of work where the skills of the computer experts – systems analysts and programmers – are much in demand to handle stock control and accounts. Retailing is a big employer but many of the jobs are part time.

PUBLIC ADMINISTRATION

Apart from the construction, manufacturing and service industries, there are two other large employers in the UK: the Civil Service and local government. The Civil Service employs people in a wide range of jobs, including clerical, secretarial, managerial and specialist staff; local government employs even more. The establishment of agencies to handle Civil Service responsibilities and, in local government, the privatisation of many services, such as hospital catering and refuse collection, and the abolition of some authorities in the large cities is changing this pattern. Many of the jobs once done by council employees are performed by contractors, sometimes the same people who were doing the job before.

THE CIVIL SERVICE

Civil servants either help to make policy or help to implement it and work for one of the 200 or so government departments or agencies. Fifty of these are based in Whitehall, and if you want a hand in making policy this is where you need to head, unless you are interested in the affairs of Northern Ireland, Scotland or Wales, which have their own regionally based offices.

If you want to be a policy implementer it is possible to work throughout the United Kingdom and sometimes abroad, if you become a diplomat for example. You need to pick an area of interest and pursue jobs when they are advertised. There is no set time of the year and it is a good idea to contact the relevant department's recruitment or personnel office to get up-to-date information. The following list identifies some of the departments seeking new recruits. If you would like to find out more about them contact the Schools and Graduate Liaison Office at the Office of Public Service, Room 127-2, The Cabinet Office, Horse Guards, London SW1P 3AL.

The Department of Health is responsible for the National Health Service. The Department of Social Security looks after child care, welfare services and social security cash benefits, such as income support. The Department of Trade and Industry promotes and assists industry, including the promotion of information technology (four laboratories are run by the Department), protects consumers, and regulates areas of industry such as insurance and radio frequencies. The Department of the Environment is concerned with local government and development, housing and construction; the Department of Transport with shipping, aviation and transport; and the Department for Education and Employment covers education and training from primary school to university level in the UK.

The Inland Revenue and Customs and Excise are both concerned with collecting taxes, and the Treasury is responsible for the control of public (ie taxpayers') money and for advising ministers on economic policy. A large spender of taxpayers' money is the Ministry of Defence, which includes the armed services: soldiers, sailors and airmen and women work in a wide range of jobs; among them are 3000 professional engineers. The Ministry of Agriculture, Fisheries and Food also employs a number of specialists in its laboratories, working on the control and eradication of animal and plant diseases, one of the main functions of the Department. Other departments include Energy; the Home Office and Lord Chancellor's Department, responsible for aspects of law and order; the Foreign and Commonwealth Office (the Diplomatic Service is now much smaller, after cutbacks in staff numbers); Royal Mint (producing coins for countries overseas as well as for the UK); the Scottish and Welsh Offices; and various smaller departments.

Civil servants are involved in management and administration as executives at various levels, or as clerical or secretarial staff, or they are employed as qualified specialists. Specialists include economists, statisticians, scientists, librarians, lawyers, accountants, architects, linguists, veterinarians, surveyors and engineers. Information about the work of the specialists and other possible degree-level work is given in booklets available from Recruitment and Assessment Services, Alençon Link, Basingstoke, Hampshire RG21 1JB; 01256 29222.

The different departments in the Civil Service recruit most of their own staff directly but they may recruit through the Recruitment and Assessment Service (RAS). Recruitment schemes are often advertised in national and local newspapers, as appropriate. Candidates with first-class degrees may apply for fast-stream admission. From these are chosen the highest level administrators.

The basic requirement for Executive Officer (EO) recruitment is normally two A levels and three GCSEs, or a degree or equivalent, but precise requirements may vary between different recruiting schemes. This applies both to general EO posts, and to specialisms such as information technology, accountancy trainee and statistical trainee.

Recruitment to Administrative Officer and Administrative Assistant clerical grade posts is carried out locally by individual government departments and agencies such as Jobcentres and careers services.

The Service, including the armed services, is in many ways like a large industrial company, with the same skills being sought, and with staff taken on at all levels. At GCSE level (or equivalent), posts will be as clerical assistants and officers, executive officers and personal secretaries, cartographic staff and Ministry of Defence technician apprentices. Some jobs need A levels – Inland Revenue valuers and student engineers, for instance. Other careers require degree-level entry.

There is a large number of applications for executive officers, the basic entry grade into the Service for those with A levels or a degree. But in fact aptitude tests whittle down the numbers (or people don't turn up for their interviews, or don't take the tests), so even those posts are not filled all that easily – which means that getting a Civil Service job is not impossible.

Because the Service is involved in advisory work, there are

31

schemes to help people keep up to date with developments in their particular field – conferences, courses, access to specialist journals, and so on – and this continuous training is one of the attractions of Civil Service work.

An advantage in the past, apart from the good training schemes and good pension prospects, of life in the Civil Service, was that it was a protected environment. This might not have suited the entrepreneurial type, who likes to make decisions and see the result of them, good or bad; there was no tangible feedback on advice, and no profit and loss account to show its final effect. However, that is changing with the introduction of agencies.

Job security used to be for life but this has all changed. You are more likely to keep your job 'if you are providing an ongoing service which the public will continue to require'. Defence contracting, for example, is decreasing, while the need for services for the old increases. Salaries are good and there is an ordered promotion system based on grades.

LOCAL GOVERNMENT

In many ways, work in local government is similar to that of the Civil Service, with staff providing support for elected councillors. There are several types of local government, but no central system; each area has its own separate structure and administration. Again, staff include administrative managers and specialists, such as librarians, architects, lawyers, engineers and accountants. But there are also other specialists not employed within the Civil Service: housing managers, recreations managers, environmental health officers, trading standards officers and town and country planning officers.

Local government work is more closely involved with the community than that of the Civil Service, so it is more possible to see the results of your work. Responsibilities of the urban, county and district councils include hospitals and social welfare, the fire, police and ambulance services, strategic planning, transportation planning, highways, traffic regulation, refuse disposal, education, museums, art galleries, physical recreation, cemeteries and parks. Administrative staff are taken on at all levels, and there are training schemes to help those who wish to progress up to senior positions – but heads of departments will be specialists, and will normally have been recruited at graduate level.

Job advertisements appear in council vacancy bulletins, local authority publications like *Opportunities*, the *Local Government Chronicle* and, mainly for graduates, the *Guardian* on Wednesdays. If you want careers and training advice try contacting the Local Government Management Board.

THE ARMED SERVICES

Like an airport, the armed services are self-supporting worlds on their own, with cooks and nurses, mechanics and typists, administrative, clerical and security staff. Skills that are useful within the services can also be in demand in civilian life, when the period of service has been completed. Some of these skills may have been learned under service training schemes, others are learned at college or university and applied to the needs of the services.

Entry is at various levels. For instance, a weapons analyst or motor transport driver needs no special academic qualifications, and both are given the necessary training. A technician can join with GCSEs, and through an apprenticeship scheme train in telecommunications, leading to BTEC or CGLI qualifications.

There are 40 different non-commissioned trades in the Royal Air Force which include engineering technician in airframe, propulsion, weapons, aircraft electrical, avionics, and synthetic trainer, and mechanics in all these specialisations as well as transport, security, air traffic control, telecommunications and aerospace systems operations. The RAF requires four GCSEs, including maths and a physics-based subject, for engineering technician apprenticeships. In the Royal Navy, engineering technicians are taken on as 'artificer apprentices' for a four-year training period and become skilled in air, marine or weapons engineering specialisations. It is possible for those who enter as technicians to be promoted to officer rank. Applicants must have GCSEs in physics or a physics-based science subject, maths and English language (or acceptable alternative), or BTEC qualifications, or have passed papers set by the Navy. Nursing recruits can enter after qualifying in the normal way but some are trained by the Navy.

Some of the skills that can be learnt may be more useful than others in later civilian life; those trained in marine engineering are less likely to find suitable work easily (because the merchant shipping fleet is getting smaller all the time) than those who have skills in communications and electronics. Entry is competitive, and there are also strict medical, nationality and residence requirements that must be fulfilled. Further details of the many specialisations, training, age limits for entry and necessary qualifications are available from the local careers information offices of each of the services.

There is a certain amount of financial help available to those who are still at school or college in the form of scholarships, bursaries and student cadetships mostly for engineering or technology-related subjects. The (very few) scholarships aim to help pay the expenses of those still at school and taking A levels for one or two years, and who, of course, intend to join one of the services; the Army has a special one-year science scholarship scheme. For those studying for a degree at a university there are bursaries and student cadetships. A bursary is paid in addition to a local education authority maintenance grant and the holders (who are still civilians while they are studying) must undertake to serve for a minimum of three years after graduating.

Undergraduate cadetship is designed for those who intend to make a career in the services, and who will serve at least 16 years after graduation; having already been commissioned as officers they receive appropriate pay and allowances until they graduate (but there is no extension for higher degrees). Naturally there is fierce competition for these awards; the services look for people with exceptional 'leadership potential' and academic qualifications. It is possible to apply for a cadetship in a final year of study, for instance for Part Two of the Engineering Council Examination.

Although you can enter the services from the age of 16, length of service dates from your eighteenth birthday. You then enter on a 22-year Open Engagement, which is pensionable, but you can claim discharge after completing two years and six months if aged 18, or after completion of initial training, but you must give up to 18 months' notice and have completed a minimum of four years' trained service. All three services are currently dispensing with senior staff and further reductions are planned.

Women in the services receive the same career opportunities as men, with the chance to train as technicians and engineers, but are unable to go into battle, serve on a submarine or be part of the mine warfare branch. Although they cannot enter the full marine corps they are able to join the Royal Marine Band. Female recruits who become pregnant can take a leave of absence and return to the same rank.

As in many other types of career, the people recruited for what are essentially the middle and top levels of management (in other words, the officers) are increasingly likely to be graduates. Half of the Army's young officers are now expected to be graduates. Apart from those who have been sponsored during their student years by bursaries or university cadetships, there are also those who go into the services after graduating as Direct Entry Graduates. Degrees may be in any discipline, although special qualifications (such as engineering) may be of more value to certain units or specialisations. As an example, an instructor in the Wrens may require a degree in engineering, maths, physics, metallurgy or computer sciences, although a small number of arts graduates may also be considered. Those with vocational degrees and work experience, such as dentists, doctors, solicitors, barristers, veterinary surgeons and ordained clergy can also be accepted as Direct Entry Graduates.

Because of the high standards expected, entry into the armed services means surviving a rigorous selection procedure involving interviews, aptitude tests, written examinations and medical examinations. Entry is particularly competitive for the more glamorous jobs, such as pilots in the Fleet Air Arm or Army Air Corps as well as in the RAF.

Once inside the self-contained world of the services, there is a ready-made social and sporting life that is seen as one of the 'perks' of a service career. Although there is less opportunity now for travel to exotic destinations, the serviceman or woman must still expect to be away from home and family for long periods.

THE POLICE FORCE

Unlike the armed services, there is no one national police force, so recruits must apply to individual forces – maybe the one in the area in which they live, or in another area that interests them. Entrance requirements vary – some forces expect four GCSEs or equivalent, including maths and English, but others rely on selection tests and medical fitness tests. Even so, all candidates now sit the new PIR (Police Initial Recruitment) test, regardless of qualifications. Like the armed services, the police have a graduate entry scheme, for which there is tough competition. In England and Wales those who apply for the scheme must already have graduated, or be in the final year of a degree course; in Scotland applications are not accepted until after graduation.

Some police forces have cadet training programmes for entrants aged 16 to 18, but the normal age for applying to join the police is $18\frac{1}{2}$, though there is no upper age limit. All who are accepted, even those on the graduate entry scheme who must apply before the age of 30, must serve a two-year probationary period as constables; graduates can then take an examination for promotion to sergeant, followed by a one-year accelerated promotion course. Training combines working on the job with academic and professional studies at the police staff college.

Although there are similarities in the training and promotion structure of the police and the armed services, police work is very different, involving constant contact with the public, from the very first day of putting on a uniform. Within the police force there are different activities, including the Criminal Investigation Department (CID), the Traffic Department, dog handler and mounted branch, river police and underwater search units. Other similar organisations are the British Transport Police and the Ministry of Defence Police.

WORLDS OF OPPORTUNITY

People talk about 'industry' as an all-embracing term and it is difficult for the outsider to imagine the various sectors within the manufacturing and service industries; however, the Department for Education and Employment has broken down these sectors, giving a picture of how the economic world as a whole is run, which may give you an idea of which branch you would like to aim for.

- The list starts at ground level, with agriculture, forestry and fishing, and horticulture as a subsidiary.
- Then energy and water supply, including coal mining, extraction of mineral oil and natural gas, oil processing, nuclear fuel production and the supply of electricity, gas and water.
- Metal manufacturing: including iron and steel, steel tubes and alloys of aluminium, copper and brass.
- Non-metallic mineral products: including products for the building industry (cement, lime, plaster, concrete), stone-working, glass and ceramic goods.
- The chemical industry: basic industrial chemicals, paints, varnishes, printing ink, pharmaceutical products, soap and toilet preparations, and specialised household products.
- Metal goods: including ferrous and non-ferrous foundries, forging, pressing and stamping, nuts, bolts and springs, metal doors and windows, and hand tools.
- Mechanical engineering: industrial plant and steelwork,

agricultural machinery and tractors, machine and small tools, components for the motor industry, industrial machinery, lifting and handling equipment, internal combustion engines (except road vehicles), compressors, refrigerating, space heating and ventilation machinery, ordnance, small arms and ammunition.
- Office machinery: data and processing equipment.
- Electrical and electronic engineering: insulated wires and cables, basic electrical and industrial equipment, telecommunication equipment (very busy), telegraph and telephone appliance equipment, radio and electronic goods, domestic electrical appliances, lighting equipment and installation of electrical equipment.
- Motor vehicles and parts: including bodies and engines, trailers and caravans.
- Other transport equipment: shipbuilding and repairing, railway and tramway vehicles, cycles and motorcycles, aerospace equipment.
- Instrument engineering: measuring and precision instruments, medical and surgical equipment, optical precision instruments, clocks and watches.
- From manufacturing the list moves on to food, drink and tobacco: meat and meat products, vegetable oils and fats, milk products, fruit, vegetable and fish processing, bread, biscuits and confectionery, and animal feedstuffs. Also spirit distilling, brewing and malting, soft drinks and tobacco.
- Textiles: including man-made fibres, covers both clothing and household textiles. It is an area with many opportunities, from manufacture to selling finished goods in the shops. Good design is needed. Includes woollen and worsted fabrics, cotton and silk, knitted goods, stockings and tights, carpets. Clothing includes footwear, hats, gloves, fur goods, men's and boys' suits, work clothing, jeans and lingerie.
- Leather and leather goods industries.
- Timber and wooden furniture: including saw-milling, planing, builders' carpentry and joinery, articles of wood and cork, wooden and upholstered furniture, shop and office fitting.
- Paper, printing and publishing: including the production of pulp, paper and board, of which consumption is increasing, packaging (which is about design as much as production), and the printing and publishing of books, magazines and newspapers.
- Rubber and plastics: including tyres, plastics for moulds, and components for colour TVs. Success in this industry depends on marketing, innovation, design and productivity improvement.
- Other manufacturing includes jewellery and coins, photo and cinematographic processing, toys and sports goods.

37

- Construction: including both construction and repair of buildings (and demolition work), civil engineering and installation of fixtures and fittings.
- Wholesale distribution is a vital industry involving the transport of agricultural and raw materials, and all the manufactured products and goods we have been considering, to their point of sale or supply.
- The next section is 'Dealing in scrap or waste materials' – fertile ground for the would-be millionaire!
- Hotels and catering: restaurants, snack bars, cafés, public houses and bars, nightclubs and licensed clubs, canteens and messes, the hotel trade and other tourist accommodation (see Leisure and entertainment, page 23).
- Repair of consumer goods: including footwear, leather and motor vehicles.
- Transport and communication: railways, sea and air transport and their supporting services, postal services, telecommunications; and storage.
- Banking, finance, insurance and business services: including estate agencies, advertising and computer services, and business services.
- Renting of construction machinery, consumer goods and transport.
- Public administration and defence: including local and national government, police, fire services, social security, refuse disposal and cleaning services, education, health services, including hospitals, nursing homes, medical practices, and social welfare.
- Recreational and cultural services: film production, radio, television, theatres, libraries, museums, art galleries, sport and other recreational services.
- Personal services: laundries, dyers and dry cleaners, hairdressing and beauty parlours.

The Department for Education and Employment, in conjunction with Radio 1, publishes *Which Way Now?* annually, designed to help school-leavers and those choosing options; it contains a useful list of occupations and qualifications.

To learn more about industry, and the specialised jobs within it, you should take advantage of any schemes run by your school and local industries to go on educational visits to factories and workshops in your area. If there is any particular aspect of it that interests you, do not be afraid to ask questions and find out more from careers libraries and the large firms themselves. Most of the larger firms have schools liaison officers or information officers, who will be very pleased to help you; or get in touch with the firm's personnel office. Careers literature sent out by companies may tend to be glossy and overstated, but will give you a good idea of their products or services.

PROFESSIONAL CAREERS

Having looked at certain sectors of industry, with special reference to the growth areas, it becomes obvious that one profession at least is very closely involved in industry – engineering; and that electrical and electronic engineers are currently particularly highly valued. However, this doesn't mean that all engineers are employed in industries producing various kinds of manufactured goods; there are also openings within bodies such as the Civil Service and local authorities for professional engineers, including electrical, mechanical and civil engineers.

Other professions also span both the manufacturing and service industries: personnel and management, accountancy and law, for example. The last two are also professions that allow the practitioner to set up his or her own consultancy business, or work for a firm specialising in accountancy or law services. The medical professions are sometimes involved in industry, but mainly as research and sometimes marketing staff. Doctors and dentists work mainly for the health service, of course, and also as private consultants, while over half of the veterinary surgeons work in their own or a colleague's private practice, and also for the Civil Service. Architects and surveyors may also have their own practices, or work for large construction companies, for the Civil Service and for local authorities. Many professions subdivide into separate specialisations.

Engineering

In the financial and business pages of the newspapers, there appear regular moans about Britain's need for more well-educated and trained graduate and technician engineers and the lack of young people coming forward for training. This is said to be due partly to the dearth of maths and physics teachers in schools (who are tempted into industry), partly to the need for more engineering and technology training in higher education and partly to what can be seen as inadequate pay and career opportunities compared with other professions. However, these problems are being looked at and should slowly be overcome, and it is hoped that engineering as a profession will eventually have the status that it already has in some countries. Since 1993 it has, of course, been easier for qualified engineers to work in EU countries, such as Germany.

There are three separate levels within the engineering profession. The topmost level is for those who have a degree from a university in engineering or a related subject – the professional engineers. Those seeking professional chartered status will soon have to achieve a postgraduate Master's qualification. This is in addition to the current rules which require professional engineers to hold an accredited honours degree, be over 25 and have two years' experience in a post with some responsibility. These rules may vary depending on the type of engineer you wish to become.

Incorporated engineers provide technical support to chartered engineers, who are generally responsible for coming up with new ideas. Quite often they will have the specific technical knowledge chartered engineers lack and may design components for a new product, operate highly complex machinery and be in charge of a team of technicians. They need a practical approach and must maintain an in-depth knowledge of the latest technological developments. Incorporated engineers are expected to hold either an NVQ level 4 or Higher National Certificate, Higher National Diploma, GNVQ level 4 or an ordinary degree and have relevant training and experience.

After the incorporated engineers come the engineering technicians. These are one step up from the technicians, or craftsmen and women, and having a more extensive technical knowledge they will undertake more responsible work, such as designing a new product if they work in a design department, carrying out detailed tests and working out production methods, as well as maintaining and repairing mechanical, electrical or measuring equipment. Their training is similar to that of the incorporated engineers, but with a more practical base.

Engineering technicians can qualify by completing a modern apprenticeship with an NVQ level 3 qualification, taking a National Diploma or Advanced GNVQ course, or by having at least two A levels. It is possible for both incorporated engineers and engineering technicians to continue with college courses, gaining a BTEC or SCOTVEC Higher National Certificate or Diploma and going on to a degree course at a university, to reach chartered engineer status. A craftsman or woman trains and qualifies either through an apprenticeship with NVQ level 2, or by taking BTEC First Certificate or Intermediate GNVQ.

Most engineers are concerned with design of equipment of some kind, research and development, and production, but there are many branches to the profession, and even within those branches there are yet more areas of specialisation.

Production engineering has become a specialised area of its own, concerned with the process of producing goods of all kinds, from fish fingers to machinery. Chemical engineers, sometimes also known as process engineers, work in industries that process materials by changing their chemical or physical state. Although originally dealing with chemicals, their work now concerns anything that is processed, as distinct from fabricated (such as machinery or tin cans), and so covers such 'flow' products as cement, paints and detergents, polymers, beer or lubricating oils. Chemical engineers have been closely involved in the petrochemical industry, but will in the future also be involved with materials (such as optical fibres) for the communications industry, and with process biotechnology, a new discipline growing out of chemical and biochemical engineering, biochemistry and microbiology, and concerned with the newer types of health care products such as monoclonal antibodies. This could be fascinating – for those who have continued their maths, physics and chemistry to A level standard. Training in chemical engineering is normally undertaken at degree level.

Graduates with degrees in engineering are currently being offered starting salaries around £12,000 to £14,000. The figure is higher for disciplines in greater demand.

Although most students doing a degree course in engineering decide at the outset which course they would prefer, it can be possible to switch to another engineering discipline during the first two years of a course. It is also possible, for those who have not studied maths and physics at A level or equivalent to take a one-year foundation conversion course at a university or college as part of a chosen engineering degree course.

Each engineering section has its own professional organisation; these are listed in *British Qualifications*, published by Kogan Page. There are about 40 in the Engineering Council, including not only the Institution of Mechanical Engineers but also organisations that would not normally spring to mind, such as the Institution of Water and Environmental Management, the Incorporated Highway Institute of Engineers, the Institution of Mining and Metallurgy, the Institution of Nuclear Engineers. Only professional engineers who are members of one of the chartered engineering institutions (they are not all chartered) can use the title 'Chartered Engineer'.

The chartered engineering institutions are: Mechanical Engineers, Production Engineers, Civil Engineers, Structural Engineers, Electrical Engineers, Electronic and Electrical Incorporated Engineers, Chemical Engineers, Gas Engineers, Mining Engineers, Mining and Metallurgy plus the Institute of Energy, the Royal Aeronautical Society, the Institute of Marine Engineers and the Royal Institution of Naval Architects.

In general, qualified engineers are needed both in the manufacturing and service industries, including the Civil Service and the Ministry of Defence, and they are also in great demand abroad; marine engineers, for example, who were unable to find suitable employment in the UK would certainly be welcomed in many countries overseas.

A proportion of qualified engineers go from university to work on the management side of an organisation, where their training in problem-solving as well as their knowledge of technology are of great value. Engineers often switch from purely engineering work to management; it is one way of preventing their becoming over-specialised in a particular area of work and of gaining promotion. Their expertise can be useful in marketing – or they may leave employment with a large firm altogether and set up their own consultancy, perhaps selling goods or engineering services overseas. Some university engineering courses are combined with aspects of management studies.

For fuller details of the type of work and prospects involved in each engineering speciality, you can write to the institutions themselves; the Engineering Council lists names and addresses.

Management and administration

A career in management does not necessarily mean working in industry; any large organisation needs an administrative structure, although the emphasis would not be the same in the different management departments of a hospital, for instance, as in a chain of retail stores. Although both would have personnel and purchasing departments, there would be no marketing and sales departments in a hospital, and no production management in either, as there would be in a manufacturing company.

There is a growing awareness in the UK of the need to recruit good management staff, particularly among the more forward-looking manufacturing companies, following the lead of Germany and Japan. Although the routes through to senior management levels still remain for people with special skills, such as engineering or accountancy, many companies will also take on university graduates and train them in management. Very often the degree subject does not matter, although with the increasing role of computers in office management, employers do usually like candidates to be numerate. This is often a way into interesting jobs for graduates with arts degrees, and they find that there is a sense of adventure and excitement in working for a competitive organisation that makes it a rewarding and satisfying career. An alternative to company management training is a postgraduate MBA (Master of Business Administration) course. A list of colleges offering management courses is available from the Institute of Management. The IM also has details of qualifications that can be gained through part-time or work-based courses, or distance learning.

Marketing is thought of as the 'sharp' end of management. It is concerned with selling products through advertising, packaging, promotions and back-up services, and with identifying the kind of products that customers might want to buy and how much they would be prepared to pay. Customers could include foreign governments, as well as shoppers in the high street. Salespeople who go 'out on the road' may have university degrees, or no special qualifications at all, depending on the company and the products, but must be prepared to travel and work unsocial hours away from home; they must be able to get on with their customers and be persuasive about the products. Language skills will become increasingly useful for marketing executives.

In a manufacturing company, the production manager is responsible for buying and storing raw materials, and for packaging, storing and finally delivering the finished product to the customer. It is a job that involves planning, organisation and coordination and keeping the plant operating efficiently, within what will normally be a fairly large department, including junior managers, who would not necessarily be expected to have degrees.

Very often people taken on in the finance department do not have any qualifications in accountancy, though they must be numerate; they are given accountancy training on the job, combined with part-time or day-release study. If they do have a degree, it may be in an arts subject. The work involves paying bills and invoicing customers, dealing with tax, national insurance and value added tax (VAT). There is also a certain amount of looking ahead to the future to fix the following year's budget, predict cash flow and fix prices. The finance department is obviously vital in any large organisation, and accountants often make it to board level.

The other important department with stable career opportunities is the personnel department. Most people imagine that it is entirely to do with looking after the welfare of the staff working within the whole organisation, and to some extent this is true; but personnel work also covers the recruitment and selection of staff, training, industrial relations (working with the trade unions represented in the company), the paying of salaries, and a certain amount of work with statistics, in planning how many staff will be needed in the future by taking into account new developments, and the number of staff who are likely to leave or change jobs. Obviously the size of an organisation, and its methods of working, make a difference to the way its personnel department is run.

Some personnel managers are recruited into the department as juniors, as wages clerks or secretaries, but nowadays most hold a degree of some kind; suitable subjects are business studies, behavioural sciences and law, but a degree in any discipline is normally acceptable. Experience in industry could also lead to personnel work. Eventually personnel managers take the Institute of Personnel Development's examinations, after relevant studies, to become members of the Institute. Some business studies degrees lead directly to IPD qualifications.

Anyone interested in a career in management can contact the local branch of the Institute of Management; it is a good idea to go along and sit in at a meeting and chat to actual managers about what they are doing – the best way to find out about any job is by talking to people who have experience of it.

Accountancy
For those who have qualified as chartered accountants, the world is virtually their oyster. Chartered accountants are well paid, they are rarely unemployed, and they can work almost anywhere in the world. Some work in industry and commerce, but most are in practice – on their own, as partners, or working in a junior role.

Other accountants, not necessarily chartered accountants, work, as would be expected, for banking and insurance companies in the financial world, in local and central government, and other areas such as management consultancy for industry and commerce.

An accountant does not have to be brilliant at maths but must at least have a good GCSE/A level pass in maths and be numerate enough to be able to acquire more mathematical expertise during the training.

Analytical ability is a subject you can't learn at school, but it is an essential one for an accountant; it means being able to think in a logical way, to sum up a situation and separate what is important and relevant from what is unimportant – it is a quality that is demanded by many professional careers, not just accountancy. Another essential is integrity, being able to keep other people's circumstances secret and confidential. This integrity is one of the reasons why qualified accountants from the UK are in demand overseas, particularly in the developing countries.

Confidentiality has to apply not only to the private individuals and small companies whose tax returns and accounts are dealt with by accountants in 'public' practice, but also to the affairs of large organisations. The accountant's advice may be sought on a wide variety of problems, and the work gives the chance of meeting and helping people involved in many different types of business.

Accountancy training is invaluable in many ways and can be used in non-accountancy jobs, such as running a business, where the financial implications of projects can be assessed on the basis of experience of business life already acquired during the training period, or in the heady financial world of the City, in the highly paid field of corporate finance, for example.

Before becoming a chartered accountant, trainees must undergo a period of training with the office of a firm of chartered accountants. First, though, they must have a degree (which can be in any discipline although most have degrees in accountancy, business, economics, science, engineering and other relevant degrees rather than subjects such as arts and languages); if the degree is in a subject such as archaeology, an additional exam would be undertaken during the early part of the training contract. Alternatively, trainees may have taken a foundation course at a university (entry requirements: five GCSE passes including maths and English language, including two A level passes or equivalent) followed by four years' training with the chartered accountancy firm. A degree course will be followed by three years' training. Occasionally HND students or members of other bodies may also be accepted for chartered accountancy training.

There are six main professional accountancy bodies who can give you further information about the various qualifications and routes into accountancy (addresses in Chapter 9).

Accounting technicians, who act as support staff for the professional chartered accountants in public practice, in industry and commerce, and in public finance, can work for the qualifications of the Association of Accounting Technicians, and can go on to become professional accountants.

Law

A degree in law is, like accountancy, useful currency in the high-flyer job market, where the skills of assessing the relevance of facts, agility of mind and of logical argument that have been gained during the training period are highly valued. However, it is not always easy to get on to a university course – A level resits are somewhat frowned upon, except under exceptional circumstances, so good results are essential.

The three-year degree course covers such subjects as Constitutional and Administrative Law, about government, the citizen and the state; Criminal Law (and later, criminology, which explores the causes of crime and its consequences); the Law of Contract, about agreements between individuals; the Legal System, about court structure, legal techniques and the role of the legal profession; the Law of Tort (civil wrongs); Land Law, concerning ownership of land; Equity and Trusts, which deals with the management and control of property to the benefit of others; Administrative Law; Commercial Law; Company Law and the Law of Partnership; Evidence; Family Law; Civil Liberties; Conflict of Laws, arising from legal problems which involve a foreign country's laws; conveyancing; jurisprudence (the search for an explanation of the nature of law); Labour Law, to do with employees, employers and trade unions; Law of the European Union; Public International Law; Revenue Law; Succession; Welfare Law.

Some of these subjects are core subjects, others will be offered only as options, and would not necessarily all be available as a choice for every student. The list does, however, give an idea of how a degree in law can be applicable to many fields of work, and gives a foundation for careers in, for instance, banking, insurance, accountancy, social work, commercial management, the Civil Service, local government, journalism, the armed services and the police. There are also degrees in combined subjects, such as law with politics, law with French, law with economics.

Graduates who want to continue in the legal profession will then study for further examinations so that they can practise as barristers or advocates (the Scottish equivalent of a barrister) or as solicitors.

Changes are proposed in the training of barristers, but at present those who want to become barristers must join one of the four Inns of Court: students can apply to join them while still at university. Graduates in disciplines other than law, with at least a second class honours degree, can undertake barrister training after completing a full-time one-year course, leading to a Common Professional Examination, at a university.

The vocational stage of a barrister's training involves a one-year Vocational course, which is heavily oversubscribed, and under half the number of applicants obtain a place. The course is organised by the Council of Legal Education at the Inns of Court School of Law at Gray's Inn in London. The Bar Examination is of a very high standard; all theoretical papers must be passed at the same sitting and only four attempts are allowed. Those who do not want to practise at the Bar can take the examination, and prepare for it part time, by private tuition, by correspondence course or at a college (details from the Council of Legal Education).

After successfully completing the Bar Examination, the barrister who intends to practise must then 'serve pupillage' for a year under pupil masters and learn about the work 'on the job'. The final, and sometimes insurmountable, hurdle for the hopeful new barrister is finding work and a place in chambers (groups of barristers to which solicitors come with 'briefs', or work, for them). There are usually around 700 pupils looking for only 200–300 places, or 'tenancies', in chambers each year. There exists, unfortunately, still an old-fashioned attitude; for many people, especially women, finding tenancies and work can prove difficult. However, this attitude is changing and some women's chambers have been established.

Some barristers earn very high sums, but others are not so successful at the Bar. Many work in industry or commerce, in organisations such as the Civil Service – or in politics. Barristers who successfully apply to become a Queen's Counsel (QC) are said to 'take silk'.

Barristers at present have to be given their work by solicitors – they don't have direct contact with the public, but this tradition may change. They specialise either in Chancery work which is concerned with such subjects as trusts, wills, conveyancing and Company Law; or Common Law work which is about criminal, family, contract and civil work. Some types involve many hours in the courts, others give rise to little court work, but a great deal of time researching and giving advice to the solicitors who seek it about special points of law. In Scotland the work of the advocate is similar to that of the barrister in England and Wales.

Solicitors go by the same name on both sides of the border, but as Scottish law is often very different they would not be working in exactly the same way.

Solicitors normally have more dealings with the public than barristers and undertake a wider range of work though they too may specialise. Broadly, they deal with conveyancing (the buying and selling of houses and other property), wills, divorce, criminal proceedings, and other problems affecting private individuals at work or in their personal lives, and they also work as consultants to commercial businesses.

Whereas practising barristers are always self-employed, solicitors in private practice normally work for a small or large firm of solicitors and would hope to move up from being an assistant solicitor to becoming a partner eventually. Again unlike barristers, who are mainly based in London, solicitors can work anywhere in the country. Those who are not in private practice will be working in the legal department of a large company or local authority, or in the Civil Service.

In theory, school-leavers can train to become solicitors but they may find it hard to find a solicitor who is willing to train them. Seventy-five per cent of entrants are law graduates who take a degree that includes the same seven core subjects needed by barristers; this is followed by a year's Legal Practice course run in a range of institutions throughout the country.

Non-law graduates follow their degrees with a one-year full-time course leading to the Common Professional Examination also taken by barristers; then they go on to take the Legal Practice course. After completing the course, graduates must then find an employer and continue training under a two-year training contract.

School-leavers and non-graduates with four GCSEs (not necessary for those over 25) train as a student member of the Institute of Legal Executives and pass papers corresponding to the seven core subjects, before attending the Legal Practice course. Over half of all solicitors now qualifying are women.

Other people who work in the legal profession, and who do not need such high entry qualifications, are barristers' clerks, justices' clerks' assistants and legal executives, who act as assistants to solicitors and may take on a great deal of responsibility within a solicitor's practice; they can train to take the examinations of the Institute of Legal Executives.

Further information on the work and training of solicitors is available from the Careers and Recruitment Service, Law Society, 227 Strand, London WC2R 1BA. Information on barristers from: The Council of Legal Education, 39 Eagle Street, London WC1R 4AJ.

The legal profession continues to change and the future will probably include more court appearances and greater specialisation for solicitors. Both the recession and new procedures for house conveyancing have had an impact on the profession, cutting new recruitment and leading to greater competition between a higher number of prospective professionals.

Surveying

To people who want to buy a house, a surveyor is the person who is sent by the mortgage company to check on the house's structure, to report on any weaknesses and to advise on its value. But there are many more sides to surveying than domestic work of this kind, with specialisations that can involve charting the sea bed, the management of farms and rural property, advising on construction projects in Africa or on North Sea oil rigs, and so on. With interests in so many activities, the profession has divided itself into seven sections, under the principal professional body, the Royal Institution of Chartered Surveyors. All surveyors must have a degree plus two years' approved practical experience (three years for quantity surveyors). In addition they must have passed the Assessment of Professional Competence before becoming members of the Institution, and therefore able to call themselves 'Chartered Surveyors'.

A chartered quantity surveyor (QS) is particularly interested in the costs of construction projects and the contracts involved, and acts as the link between client, architect, civil or structural engineer and builder. A QS is consulted right at the beginning of a project – which might be a building, a motorway, the accommodation module of an offshore oil platform, telephone exchanges in Africa, or a hospital in the Middle East – to estimate the possible costs. The costs are monitored during construction until all the accounts have been paid, after completion. Another aspect of the work is calculating the possible costs of a project for a client who wants to tender, or bid, for the work – and as the amounts offered in a tender must be secret, the work has to be highly confidential. Increasingly, QSs are becoming project managers, in charge not only of the costs on a project, but of all the various specialists and consultants involved in it, including the architects.

Surveyors can also work on construction projects overseas where their skills are much in demand. They are recruited to work on short-term contracts of a few weeks to up to three years and many have become highly mobile, gaining experience and promotion in different companies, on different projects.

Many QSs have their own firm as a private practice, others are employed by local authorities or the Civil Service, or within building and civil engineering companies.

Building surveyors work in private practices, which vary in size from small to very large, in commercial firms of all kinds as consultants in charge of the maintenance of the buildings, and for local authorities or the Civil Service. The work is extremely varied, concerned not only with the construction of new buildings, but with the maintenance and restoration of old ones. They arrange for contractors to carry out the work, deal with a wide range of legal and technical problems and often also do a certain amount of architectural design. Building surveyors are the ones who carry out surveys for someone thinking of buying a house, and will also advise a house-owner on, for example, a leaking roof – so there can be a great deal of contact with the general public (and a certain amount of crawling into loft spaces looking for dry rot, or over roofs looking for loose slates on a cold or windy day!). Building surveying is a growing profession and, like quantity surveying, offers the chance of gaining experience with different employers and becoming a project manager.

Land or hydrographic surveyors, like quantity surveyors, are much in demand abroad. Land surveyors are the people you see at the side of the road using a theodolite to help with the planning of construction works, or to monitor structures for movement – they are concerned with taking precise measurements and must work to demanding standards of accuracy, using sophisticated equipment including computers both on site and in the office. Hydrographic surveyors make charts of the sea bed and surface features within ports, coastal waters, shipping lanes and deep sea areas. This can involve them in offshore oil and gas projects and mineral resources development, and they often work outside British waters, though they are also employed by port authorities and the Navy.

Valuation is the special skill of a general practice surveyor who assesses the value of property for mortgages, for insurance brokers, estate agents, rating or tax offices, or for people wanting to invest in property. Some specialise in the valuation of furniture or works of art, or plant and machinery. It is work that has a more commercial bias than other types of surveying.

The three remaining specialities are: land agents or agricultural surveyors, working mainly in private practice in a rural environment, and concerned with farm stock as well as property; minerals surveyors, involved in various aspects of mining and mineral workings; and planning and development surveyors, mainly employed by local government or private practice, who work on both urban and rural planning.

Most surveyors train by taking university degree courses in their chosen sector, or by taking a degree or diploma in a non-specialist subject. Details on training for RICS qualifications are available from the Education and Training Department, the Royal Institution of Chartered Surveyors. The two other organisations who offer qualifications are the Faculty of Architects and Surveyors and the Incorporated Association of Architects and Surveyors.

Another possible route into surveying is as a surveying technician, who would be taken on as a school-leaver with four GCSE passes including maths, English and science or equivalent, to work under the supervision of a chartered surveyor. Technicians can gain a great deal of practical experience and technical knowledge working in private practice, commerce, the Civil Service or local authorities, and may rise to senior positions, becoming partners in private practice, or managers and heads of departments elsewhere. They would study part time for BTEC or SCOTVEC awards and become members of the Society of Surveying Technicians after taking a Joint Test of Competence operated by the SST and RICS; they could also eventually become members of the Royal Institution of Chartered Surveyors.

Architecture
Architects are concerned with every aspect of building, from where to site the lavatories to how a huge office block will look on the skyline, and with both artistic effects and the down-to-earth decisions about building materials to be used and how to make the project cost-effective for the client.

They are consulted about new office buildings, shopping developments and private housing. Clients are mainly from the private sector because there is less public money available for

51

schools, public sector housing and hospitals. As well as designing new buildings, architects also direct the alteration, renovation and extension of old ones.

Architects can work on a number of types of building, from sewage farms, power stations and hospitals for government and local authorities, to pubs, shops, laboratories and mosques. As well as the restoration of old buildings, some of which can be of great historic interest, demanding the knowledge of old skills and materials, they can also be involved in town planning, interior design, and even landscape design.

Architects work in private practices, some very large; in the architects' departments of local authorities or in the Civil Service; or on a collective basis in an architects' cooperative.

The training is long, taking seven years at least before registration as an architect and membership of the Royal Institute of British Architects. It includes three years studying for a degree in architecture, and two years' study for a further degree or diploma in architecture, interspersed with at least two years' practical experience.

Medicine

Medicine is a career that everyone knows about in a general kind of way, because they will certainly have met a doctor at some time. But there are many specialisations that the qualified doctor can follow, apart from becoming a family doctor, or general practitioner (GP). The first major decision is whether to specialise in medicine, which is to do with preventing and treating illness, or in surgery. Hospital specialties in medicine include paediatrics (work with children), cardiology, geriatrics (old people), respiratory diseases, and some 12 others. Other more general hospital specialties are accident and emergency work, anaesthesia, obstetrics and gynaecology, pathology (the study of disease), psychiatry, diagnostic radiology and radiotherapy. Apart from general surgery, surgeons may specialise, too; the largest and still growing surgical speciality, with good career prospects, is that of orthopaedics (bones) and traumatology. Qualified doctors also become specialists in community medicine, and others go into occupational medicine, the armed services, the pharmaceuticals industry, full-time research and other work connected with medical sciences.

Although doctors are never likely to be unemployed, they may not always be able to get the kind of post they feel is ideal; they may want general practice work in a pleasant country town, but many have to settle for a practice in a deprived inner city environment instead or work outside the medical profession. Or they may not be able to specialise in obstetrics as they would like, but find there is a great need for specialists in geriatric medicine, including psychiatry, to work with the growing numbers of elderly people. After completing three years' vocational training after registration as a doctor, a GP is able to earn a higher income than a hospital doctor, and will also have a settled home.

Training is long, five or six years, and demanding, with high entry qualifications needed. There are examinations after the first and second years of training, at which point many students fall by the wayside – sometimes because the academic standard required is too great for them to cope with, and sometimes because motivation is not strong enough – parents are sometimes more keen on their offspring becoming doctors than the offspring themselves. 'Learning medicine', £6.95 available from the British Medical Association Bookshop at Burton Street, London WC1H 9JR, and the BMA's own careers leaflets, give helpful advice about training and specialisation.

Training to be a dentist is also long – four to five years. Most then enter general practice, and can achieve high earnings, although the possibility of the discovery of an agent that will prevent caries (the disease that causes dental decay) could change the way dentists work and put more emphasis on cosmetic dentistry in the future. Dentists enter general practice as assistants or associates, and later buy into a partnership or set up on their own – which can be expensive. Dentists also work for the community dental service, which includes school, maternity and child welfare work, and in hospitals, the armed services and large commercial companies. They also do lecturing and research work.

The recommended target net income for practice work, 1993–94, was set at £36,352; salaries for Community Dental Officers range from £19,320 to £28,390; a top hospital consultant would receive about £51,165 plus merit award; salaries in the armed services are from £26,733 to £53,502. The recommended increase for 1994–95 was 3 per cent.

Three good A level passes are needed for training as a dental surgeon; a dental hygienist, who works with a dentist, trains for one year and needs at least five GCSE passes or equivalent, as well as general training as a dental surgery assistant; a dental surgery assistant or dental nurse, as they are also known, needs no academic qualifications and can take a one- to two-year full-time course or study part time for a National Certificate. Both dental hygienists and dental surgery assistants can also work in hospitals or the other areas in which dentists practise. Other careers associated with dentistry are those of dental technicians, who make up dental appliances (such as false teeth) and are trained by apprenticeship combined with day-release courses for up to five years in a commercial laboratory, or in the laboratory of a dental practice, hospital or health authority; and there are also full-time college BTEC courses. College entry requirements are five GCSE passes including two science subjects, maths and English, or equivalent.

The final member of the dental team is the dental therapist or auxiliary, who works in local authority clinics and hospitals – not in general practice surgeries – and may carry out simple dental treatments and give advice on dental care. The course lasts two years full time based in London; candidates need five GCSE passes or equivalent. Salaries can rise to £16,678.

The address of the General Dental Council is 37 Wimpole Street, London W1M 8DQ for information about training and salaries.

The Council for Professions Supplementary to Medicine (CPSM), Park House, 184 Kennington Park Road, London SE11 4BU, covers seven other professions which do not demand the same high entry qualifications to training as do medicine and dentistry, but are involved in caring for the health of individuals and the community. These are chiropody/podiatry (concerned with the health of feet, often particularly helping elderly people); dietetics (dietitians give advice on diet within the community as well as helping very sick people, and can also work within industry); occupational therapy, helping people who are mentally or physically handicapped to become self-reliant; orthoptics, treating abnormalities and weaknesses in the eye, often working with young children; physiotherapy, helping people who are physically disabled through illness, such as a stroke, or through injury, perhaps caused by a car accident, to regain as much strength and mobility as possible through exercises and manipulation (also includes remedial gymnastics, involving games and recreational exercise, often working with children, including those with physical disabilities, or in industrial rehabilitation centres); radiography, either taking X-rays of patients for diagnosis by doctors and surgeons, or giving radiotherapy treatment to cancer patients; medical laboratory sciences, which involves laboratory work and principally attracts science graduates with an honours degree, although school-leavers with five GCSE passes (including science and English language) or equivalent can apply for training.

As well as working for the NHS, laboratory scientists also work for the Public Health Laboratory Service, the Medical Research Council, blood transfusion services, in laboratories in manufacturing firms (such as those producing pharmaceutical products), government departments, forensic laboratories, the Health and Safety Executive and the armed services. Further details about all these professions can be obtained from the relevant associations (addresses from the CPSM). There are also work and training opportunities in laboratories such as those mentioned above for laboratory technicians; minimum qualifications are normally GCSE passes, although some employers may accept lower grades.

It should be borne in mind that although minimum grades may be low, there is competition for entry to training in these professions and those with good qualifications have a better chance of being accepted.

Other people who work within the health and medical services include speech and language therapists (in demand at the moment), nurses, midwives and health visitors (training details from the Royal College of Speech and Language Therapists, 7 Bath Place, Rivington Street, London EC2A 3DR and the English National Board for Nursing, Midwifery and Health Visiting, Careers Advisory Centre, Victory House, 170 Tottenham Court Road W1P 0HA).

Working within the Health Service is not necessarily well paid, except at the top end of the medical profession, and the availability of jobs is affected by government funding. However, there are opportunities in the private sector – there is always a need for health care and there will increasingly be a demand for people to work with the elderly.

Alternatives to conventional medicine have found new markets recently and treatments such as homoeopathy and acupuncture have increased in popularity. Kogan Page publish *Working in Complementary and Alternative Medicine* for those interested in this area of work.

GRADUATE EMPLOYMENT

Medicine is one of the subjects, along with accountancy, civil engineering and architecture, where new graduates are bound to be employed immediately after leaving their university because the training they have to undergo after graduation incorporates a period of employment. However, the fact that they can find places to train means that there is interest in their qualifications, and they are likely to find work in the longer term as well. Veterinary science is another subject that has virtually no unemployment because the limited number of college places restricts the intake of graduates accepted for training, keeping the numbers within the profession constant. And, of course, graduates in the engineering disciplines, maths and the business-related sciences, such as computer science, are likely to be snapped up by employers straight away.

At the other end of the scale, there are subjects where the initial unemployment rate is high, even for graduates. These are subjects such as zoology, biology, biochemistry, English, arts, languages and arts/languages combinations, drama, history, philosophy, geography. Some seemingly similar subjects show differences in employment, too. For instance, pharmacy/pharmacology graduates are more in demand than chemistry graduates, and among engineers, graduates in production engineering have better chances than chemical engineers. However, skill in mathematics is something that employers look for, so those whose discipline embraces maths in some form can do postgraduate training in a business- or computer-related studies course or train in accountancy. An up-to-date guide is given in 'Current Vacancies' and 'Statistical Quarterly', published by the Central Services Unit (Publications) Ltd, Armstrong House, Oxford Road, Manchester M1 7ED.

Postgraduate training is often the answer for first-degree graduates who do not go into some kind of employment. Some, especially scientists, may continue studying their subject, taking a one-year master's degree or a PhD (usually three years) because employers expect the higher qualification. A PhD would be used for an academic career, or for a research job in private industry or government, but sponsorship or grants are necessary and fewer grants are available now. All teacher training, including School-Centred Initial Teacher Training (SCITT), is eligible for a grant and a PGCE (Postgraduate Certificate of Education) is a designated course.

Doing postgraduate training or study gives graduates who have degrees that are not in themselves attractive to employers the opportunity to acquire new skills that they can use effectively. Many, for instance, do training in accountancy, although their degree may have no relevance to financial work at all. Employers look on any degree as an indication that the person has the ability to study, to think constructively, to work on their own and to exercise critical judgement. Combining a degree with a course in business studies, such as a one-year MBA (Master of Business Administration) course in business management, or computer skills will very often lead to jobs in management.

Business administration and management is a field that graduates from all kinds of discipline may eventually enter, whether their degree is in the sciences, social sciences, languages or other arts. Even a company whose products are chemically-based will recruit non-science graduates to work in the marketing department; a degree in history could be just as useful in that context as one that is science-based.

The company would probably give a period of further training and the graduate would go into marketing, selling, buying, computer programming, systems analysis or personnel – or into some kind of clerical, secretarial or management support work.

Linked with industry and commerce are other service areas that attract graduates, such as advertising, market research, public relations and purchasing.

Graduates with various types of degree, not necessarily maths-based, may be recruited straight into banking or insurance, where they would be given appropriate training – or they may prefer to do postgraduate training in accountancy first.

Legal training is also popular among graduates – they may continue with a legal career, or they may use it as a useful qualification in the job market.

Teacher training has been a traditional route for many graduates who were unable to find a suitable job, or were undecided about what to do. There are now fewer places and more competition for them, and except in such subjects as maths, physics, chemistry, craft, design and technology, and modern languages, less certainty of finding work easily, especially in a pleasant environment, if they do decide to make teaching their career.

Further study or training is a good way of gaining time while deciding about a career choice – but it is obviously a good idea to undertake the type of training that will be of use later, rather than continuing with research into a subject that has no currency in the job market and may not lead to a lecturing post either.

Other fields in which employers tend to take on graduates are: radio and television, journalism, retailing, marketing and the

Civil Service. Social and welfare work is another possibility, as it takes people of all disciplines, not just, as one might have thought, those with a degree in sociology.

The type of employment graduates find is changing. Few people dare to predict what recruitment will be like in the future but a number of trends can be seen. The first is short-term employment or unemployment following graduation. Many graduates take short-term employment as a stopgap to pay off the substantial debts they accrue at university. (Barclays Bank estimate that about 80 per cent leave with debts, the average being about £2000.) Others do so because their chosen company only offers fixed-term contracts. Employment is expected to be much more flexible and less secure, with many graduates expected to move between jobs and projects which demand of them a specific quality.

Unemployment among new graduates is high and, because almost twice as many people graduated last year than in 1985, competition for jobs will get harder. Even so, unemployment among graduates is still proportionally lower than it is for the rest of the population, suggesting that over a working life graduates statistically still have a better chance of finding work and keeping it than non-graduates.

Graduates are increasingly being asked to perform non-graduate jobs as the competition gets stiffer and some will be disappointed by the employment they find. On the whole, however, the rewards for graduates are still high. Starting salaries are better than they were and new patterns of working are likely to make the future very interesting for those who are determined to seek out new opportunities.

It shouldn't be thought, however, that going into higher education after school is solely about finding a good job – that can be achieved in other ways. Higher education gives the student the chance to continue studying a favourite subject in greater depth, or learn about a new one that is not taught at school. It also means getting involved in a variety of clubs, activities and interests, meeting like-minded people and making friendships that will perhaps last for many years. At college, students learn how to express ideas and make critical analyses, and get used to the habit of study – useful qualities. This is why it can be better to choose a subject that will be a pleasure and challenge to study – rather than going for one that may have good employment potential but will be a misery to study because you do not enjoy it, and will probably dislike any job it leads to afterwards.

Graduates should also realise that while employers look upon a degree as being evidence that they have a bright, hard-working and mature candidate sitting in front of them at an interview, they are also looking for people with the right personality for the job.

PATTERNS OF WORKING

Job seekers in the 1990s face a different world from that of their predecessors. Employment patterns change every decade and there is no sure way of predicting the future. In the 1960s Britain had a very strong industrial workforce and full employment. Now this is past history and we celebrate the heritage of industrialisation, rather than its practice. Britain is often described as a post-industrial nation, but what does that mean?

In employment terms Britain will never again employ the same levels of coal miners, steel workers, factory workers and even clerical staff as it did in the 1960s. Instead, it will import these types of product, or rely on newer technologies like information technology or more efficient materials like gas.

The early 1980s were characterised by industrial decline and mass unemployment, the mid-1980s by a boom in service-related industries like banking, insurance and retailing, and the late 1980s by slow economic growth rates and the end of the boom.

At the same time southern counties benefited from a new wave of technological development and new jobs were created in light industries like information technology. Some cities became famous for their growth, especially Peterborough and Swindon, both of which were ideally situated to make the most of motorway links to London and the rest of the country.

The 1990s have seen patterns of work change again. The recession forced prosperous companies to 'downsize' their operations and cut jobs while less prosperous companies closed completely. The unemployment which had characterised the early 1980s was back again and once more the recession coincided with a new wave of technological development which reduced numbers of clerical staff further.

Now the workforce is expected to be flexible, competitive, well trained and mobile. This could mean moving to a new area to find work, which you may view as either a dismal prospect or a great challenge. Either way, mobility is a very useful asset when job hunting and can lead to interesting and highly paid work.

Another aspect of mobility which has become a feature of employment recently is moving from one job to another. It used to be fairly certain that once an employee had joined a company, there would perhaps be a steady progression up the promotion ladder but no change of employer until the day the gold watch was handed over on retirement. This is no longer the case: as redundancies began to force people to change jobs, mobility became the rule. The average manager tends to change jobs around four times now, and doing so can be the only way to gain promotion and higher pay. Only one in ten will stay with the same job all their lives, and this pattern is true of the workforce generally. Although too many changes of job could indicate the unsuitability of a candidate for a new job, an employer who is recruiting new staff would see a certain amount of movement between jobs as showing that the candidate has been willing to gain experience in different departments or activities, and has avoided the cul-de-sac of overspecialisation.

Changing jobs may mean moving to another company, but could also mean moving between different departments of the same firm: it really is a question of taking opportunities as they arise, in the hope that they will lead to whatever goal the individual has decided to work towards.

One problem in switching jobs between different companies is that doing so can affect pensions – this may not seem to matter to a young person, but it begins to be more important to people in their early thirties. However, the new personal pension schemes can be taken with you from job to job and are an alternative to company pension schemes.

People not only move around to gain experience or promotion within the same type of job, but may make drastic career changes too. A number of well-known faces on television started out as teachers or doctors; some who are now teachers have moved across from the business world. Other former company employees have started up their own businesses, either providing services for the same industry, or moving into something completely different – running a restaurant or pub, perhaps. People with professional qualifications who have been employed within large consultancy firms may break away and start up on their own, where they have greater decision-making freedom and the chance of a higher income.

SELF-EMPLOYMENT

About 13 per cent of people are self-employed, with two-thirds working in the service sector. People are more likely to take the plunge into running their own business as they get older. A large group of self-employed people is 'managerial' in wholesale and retail distribution. Another large group has craft and similar occupations – people who have set up on their own to make and sell, for instance, items of jewellery, pottery, handmade furniture or perhaps musical instruments. Self-employment has increased most dramatically among women, especially in the personal services of catering, cleaning and hairdressing.

Companies are now reluctant to pay people regular wages through their payroll when they can buy in contractors when a specific job needs doing. This allows self-employed people to move between jobs, and while it may be a risky option those who have made a name for themselves for doing good work will be hired regularly.

For many people self-employment is a way of getting back to work after periods of unemployment. For others it is a way of carrying on work that they used to do for an employer. The tendering out of council work to contractors has led to the formation of a number of small companies whose owners charge a fee, rather than take a wage.

As a way both of cutting unemployment and promoting the entrepreneurial spirit and, it is to be hoped, some healthy new businesses, the government offers both financial and advisory help to people wanting to set up on their own through Training and Enterprise Councils (TECs) in England and Wales or Local Enterprise Councils (LECs) in Scotland. The main role of the TECs is to assess training needs of local businesses, and offer training schemes through companies and colleges. One of their responsibilities is to offer advice and guidance for people who want to start their own business. This includes enterprise-awareness events, designed to give would-be entrepreneurs an idea of what it is like to be self-employed and setting up in business; also enterprise training, in skills such as accounting and marketing; business advice and counselling, and access to the support needed in setting up a business; and a free business planning kit, backed up with professional support combined, if necessary, with a business training course either free or at special rates. There are tax-relief arrangements for those who spend their own money on training courses and exams.

TECs can be contacted through local Jobcentres. Companies that give business training are listed in the Yellow Pages under Enterprise Agencies. Or contact Business in the Community, 8 Stratton Street, London W1X 5FD.

Training vouchers or credits towards training may be available from the local TEC. As TECs operate independently, there are no countrywide guidelines as to the services and financial support that must be offered – so persistence may be needed to get all the benefits possible (useful early business training).

The old Enterprise Allowance, which paid £40 for up to 52 weeks while a business was getting established, has been discontinued, but financial support along the same lines, known as Business Start-up, may be available from the local TEC – another case for persistence.

In Scotland, the Scottish Enterprise Foundation is a unit within the University of Stirling that aims to promote a spirit of enterprise through research and training in the fields of new business creation and the development of small businesses. It provides programmes for undergraduates and postgraduate students of the university; training for women and graduate business start-ups; management training with an emphasis on exporting; and support through its resource centre for agencies that provide help to small businesses. The university also offers an MSc in Entrepreneurial Studies. Contact the Scottish Enterprise Foundation, University of Stirling, Stirling FK9 4LA.

Part 2

2. What Do You Want from a Career?

Look around objectively at the people you know: friends, parents of friends, your own parents and their friends, relations and other people you meet, such as teachers, people in shops, the bank manager, the mechanic who services the family car. Putting all these innocent specimens under the microscope can help you quite a bit in deciding what you want to do with your life. Even if the job they do is not one that appeals to you from what you know about it, finding out more from them about exactly what it is they do (and it's amazing how ignorant people can be even about what their parents' jobs entail) could help a lot. Perhaps the work is more interesting and fulfilling than it seems – or maybe it appears to be fascinating but is in reality deadly dull. Think about their lifestyle too, where and how they live and whether it bears any approximation to the way you would eventually like to be living.

HOW DO YOU SEE YOURSELF LIVING WHEN YOU ARE 30?

Maybe you find it hard to imagine yourself at perhaps twice the age you are now. And, of course, as you learn more about the type of work that people do and the way people live, through making new friends as you get older, your ideas and ideals will change. But getting some picture in your mind now of the way you would like to live could give shape to your career pattern and make the first steps seem clearer.

Maybe you would like to be a lone rolling stone, working as a game warden in Africa, or nursing in the Middle East, or working as a croupier in some exotic holiday spot. Anything is possible, but it is more probable that by the time you are 30 you will have married, will perhaps have children, and be living in a rented or mortgaged house or flat. Would you like it to be in the town or the country, to have a garden, or even a swimming pool? If this is the case, you will have to put in some hard work beforehand to earn the kind of money that a swimming pool requires – either as a financial whizz-kid in the City, or as a qualified professional working in an area where your expertise is much in demand.

You will have to decide whether you wish to live in a city or town, making a choice of lifestyles and deciding whether you will be able to satisfy your greatest loves if you take a job in a particular location. Mountain climbers tend to be happiest where there are mountains and theatre goers need to live close to a cultural centre. Of course, there is no guarantee that you will have the same interests all your life and many people move from the city to the country and vice versa.

If spare-time interests are very important to you – perhaps you are an amateur sports referee at weekends – then you will need to decide on the kind of job that will allow you to carry on with these activities. It may not be a high-flying 'living to work' type of job but more of a safe 'working to live' one.

IN AN OFFICE IN A LARGE ORGANISATION?

Many of the 'safe' jobs are within large commercial organisa-tions, in local government or the Civil Service at the technical or secretarial level. They don't involve stress or the 'whose head on the chopping block?' uncertainty of the higher managing and marketing levels and give you regular hours and the ability to leave the work behind you when you go home, so that you can enjoy your leisure-time activities to the full.

Working in an office usually means working as part of a team or group of others, sticking to routine and learning to cope with 'office politics' and people you may not like. This is just as true of a research laboratory as it is of a typing pool or accounting department in a large firm.

WORKING IN A PROFESSIONAL PRACTICE

Doctors in general practice work for the National Health Service, although they may also undertake treatment of private patients, while consultants may be entirely within the private sector. Dentists work for the NHS or in a private capacity. On the other hand, other professionals such as accountants, solicitors, archi-tects, surveyors or veterinary surgeons are in effect working in an independent small business if they go into a practice. The newly qualified person will begin as an assistant in a practice and may move around to several practices to gain experience in various types of work before becoming a junior partner in a practice with one or more principal partners, finally becoming a principal partner. Buying into a partnership can involve an outlay of money either in a lump sum or paid off over several years. Alternatively, a professional person may set up in practice alone perhaps later taking on one or more partners if the volume of work justifies it.

Being a partner in a professional practice can involve a great deal of work: getting known in the local area by becoming involved in local activities and committees, being prepared to work, sometimes unpaid, in the evenings and at weekends, and making sure that high standards are maintained within the practice. Business acumen is needed to hire and fire staff, keep up to date with accounts, chase bad debts and deal with tax matters. Knowledge of running a business is not a subject that is covered in most university courses for the professions; realising how necessary it is can be something of a surprise to newly qualified graduates.

TOWN OR COUNTRY?

Qualified professionals in general practice, and those working with them, can choose to work anywhere in the country; even veterinary surgeons, whom one would expect to find mostly in rural communities, can not only set themselves up in the centre of towns, running small-animal practices, but can do better financially in an urban practice. So, although a small country town may seem an attractive and ideal place to carry on a professional business, further research may show that there is not enough work in the area to justify a practice there – especially if there are other similar ones in the area.

With some types of work there is virtually no choice: many types of banking and financial services are carried on solely in the City and most media activity is centred in London or other large towns; this includes a great deal of radio and television work, journalism, advertising, public relations and theatrical entertainment.

Some industry is still closely linked with large towns but, as in the electronics industries, there is a trend for industry to move away from the cities (which accounts for a great deal of inner city decay) and for newer ones to be grouped around smaller towns, such as Milton Keynes, in areas where there are good transport links. The service industries, such as retailing, have followed these shifts in population and jobs, with large hypermarkets often built on the edge of towns rather than in the centre, although new legislation looks set to put an end to new out-of-town shopping centre developments.

New trends in information technology also mean that many office jobs can be carried on at home, using machines linked to a main office, so that an office in a town would need to be visited only occasionally, instead of every day.

This new way of work, often called telecottaging, allows individuals to live and work in rural areas. The Internet, with its 30 million users, and multi-media software, look likely to hasten the advance of this type of work. Some developers are even planning housing estates specifically for rural computer users.

DO YOU WANT TO EARN A LOT OF MONEY?

This may seem at first to be a silly question but, as they say, money isn't everything. Some of the people who earn large amounts in their twenties in the City or in advertising are often considered to have 'burnt out' in their thirties, and do not do so well later. Certain types of work, such as advertising and, to some degree, management, look for young talent and so one cannot assume that high earnings will last until retirement – although earnings in top industrial management can be very high indeed, as can earnings in the City among corporate finance directors, insurance actuaries, investment analysts (around £180,000), futures specialists and others.

Qualified professionals, self-employed or in partnerships, can be making up to £370,000 annually (partner in a top firm of accountants); barristers, either self-employed (as most are) or in industry, and hospital consultants can be among the top earners (£250,000). Other professional careers that can lead to a high income, even on leaving university, are those that are in demand, such as electronics engineers, computer specialists, or successful marketing executives and finance directors. These are all jobs that demand a great deal of commitment to earn the high returns with perhaps only a limited amount of time to spend with the family and on leisure activities. It can mean being the first into the office in the mornings and the last to leave at night, with weekend work as well.

Compared with many careers the Civil Service pays good salaries to those in the higher grades. They may not have the 'perks', such as company car, children's education (for workers overseas), luncheon vouchers and medical insurance (or cheap mortgages for those with jobs in banks, insurance companies and building societies), that people working in industry and the private sector may have, but they do have very good pension schemes. Finding out about perks and pension schemes is part of the research that should be done before deciding on a job.

Some work, such as teaching and lecturing, and dentistry, may have good initial salaries, but offer no scope for improvement later – in teaching it is difficult to move up from one grade to the next, and even head teachers, except those in large schools, do not have salaries that compare favourably with those for heads of departments in the Civil Service.

A SAFE BET OR A GAMBLE?

It is normally accepted that working for yourself gives the best chance of very high earnings – but with greater risks than working within a large organisation. You can aim to do so after working as a professional with a company and gaining experience, so that you can set up a consultancy business using your knowledge and contacts. Or you may decide to manufacture a product for which you have spotted a market, or provide a service which you know is in demand.

There are risks of bankruptcy attached to running any business and you must take into account extra costs such as those for private pension schemes, life assurance, medical insurance, and the keeping of proper accounts for tax purposes. If there is sudden turnaround in what seemed like a booming market, you could lose everything you have invested; equally, you could become a millionaire.

DO YOU HAVE A YEN FOR TRAVEL?

It is not as easy to work overseas (outside the European Union) as it used to be. Residence visas and work permits are required by most countries, and they are only likely to look favourably on people whose skills they need: secretarial, nursing and other medical qualifications are welcomed; so are qualified engineers, scientists and craft technicians if there is a shortage of suitable qualified nationals. Where there are enough qualified nationals, outsiders will not be allowed in to take jobs from them. This applies to employees of multinational companies, such as airlines, as well as local companies, except occasionally at top management level and in certain skill areas. People may go abroad on a short contract, perhaps for three months, to handle a specific job; or for a two- to three-year period working for a UK-based company or for an employer abroad. Asia and Australia have the most expats.

Employees of large companies who work overseas permanently are mainly marketing executives, who may be responsible for one enormous area such as the whole of South-East Asia and the Far East, including the Pacific Rim, which is now one of the most important financial and industrial centres in the world. Cities like Tokyo and Singapore have taken on a new significance as millions of stocks and shares are traded every day. Britain's biggest investment banks have offices in both these cities and can win and lose vast amounts of money.

Some hopefuls going overseas on the chance of finding work may be able to do so teaching English, becoming a guide (though some knowledge of the language would be necessary), doing secretarial work, or becoming a part-time newspaper correspondent, but there is little likelihood of earning very much money.

Teaching English as a Foreign Language is a recognised qualification which allows the holder to work all over the world. Many graduates choose this option as a way of travelling around the world before settling down to a job at home.

If you wish to work with children, but not as a teacher, it is also possible to find work in America and Canada as a summer camp leader. The work is tough and only lasts for a few months in the summer, but it could provide you with the opportunity to travel through North America.

There are many other ways to travel the world. Expeditions and environmental projects are becoming increasingly popular for the adventurous, but as most of them ask for a financial contribution you have to raise your own funds and they can be quite expensive.

Many school and college leavers take time out to see the world before they settle down into a more routine occupation. Others leave, get used to the lifestyle and don't bother coming back for years. Either way, travel has become a popular option for those seeking to broaden their horizons.

If you do have a yen for travel, research your trip well in advance and make the most of your journey. Read up on the subject; like any other occupation, travellers have their own tricks of the trade. Of course, only a few make it their genuine occupation but travel can give you a head start at job interviews if your prospective employer is looking for someone who is willing to show initiative.

Many people go overseas with one of the aid agencies, such as the VSO (Voluntary Service Overseas), ODA (Overseas Development Administration), the UN and others. They will go on a two- or three-year contract basis and, again, countries will not accept anyone without the qualifications and experience they are looking for – medical, civil engineering, veterinary or teaching specialities.

A problem of overseas work is the splitting of families if it is not possible for partner and children to live in the country (perhaps because it is dangerous); often there is little for wives to do, except run nursery schools, unless they also have qualifications that are acceptable to the host country. Many people with families return home when children are in their early teens – so working overseas need not necessarily be permanent. However, those returning can find that they have lost touch with advances in technology or changes in their company's organisation, and that they no longer have the freedom of decision-making that they were used to abroad.

THE SINGLE MARKET

Closer to home, many companies will become more involved in Europe as a result of the single market, which removes all barriers to trade within the European Union and allows the free movement of goods, services, capital and people. It also allows professional qualifications gained in one country to be recognised in another; NVQs are being developed with the aim of their being easily recognised as qualifications across the EU.

However, these qualifications may not be enough to clinch a job across the Channel if the candidate does not also have the necessary language skills – unless there is no one else in line for the job who has the right credentials.

The four freedoms described above will soon be extended to European countries which are not members of the European Union but do form part of a wider group of states, known as the European Economic Area. This group incorporates Eastern European countries, Switzerland, Norway and other countries which have close trading links with the EU. This means that Britons will be able to move freely between 28 countries.

In all these countries a qualified professional of one member state is recognised as a fully qualified professional in another.

Having said this, British professionals tend to be at a disadvantage unless they have several years' working experience. This is because recent graduates, of whom only 2 per cent start their working lives in Europe, complete degree courses which are much shorter than their European counterparts. Many European companies consider a 21-year-old to be without the correct management training. For this reason those teaching English in Europe tend to make up most of that 2 per cent.

In addition, European companies expect graduates to be able to offer relevant vocational knowledge. It is not enough to have studied any degree and expect training when you arrive in Europe. Instead, those wanting to work in Europe should consider a vocational degree and quite possibly a postgraduate degree. It is also possible to take a degree in Britain with a European bias that allows the student to spend one year of the course in another country. There is an increasing demand for management graduates who can operate at a European level.

ERASMUS (European Community Action Scheme for the Mobility of University Students), now part of the new SOCRATES programme, helps students to study in other EU countries for periods of 3–12 months. For further information contact your chosen university, UK ERASMUS Student Grants Council, The University, Canterbury, Kent CT2 7PD, or write to the Department for Education and Employment for their booklet *The European Choice – A Guide to Opportunities for Higher Education in Europe*; the address is DFE Publications Centre, PO Box 2193, London E15 2EU.

Information on job vacancies within the EU is handled by the Overseas Placing Unit in Sheffield through local Jobcentres.

Anyone considering studying or working abroad, even if it is only for a short period as part of a wider travel plan, should contact the Central Bureau for Educational Visits and Exchanges. They publish a number of useful books and pamphlets and will help you to get to grips with new training programmes like Leonardo da Vinci.

DO YOU SEE YOURSELF WORKING INDOORS OR OUT OF DOORS?

Those who fancy the idea of striding the fields as a farmer will unfortunately have to think again – unless their family already owns a farm that they could hope to inherit, or they think they know someone who will give them a job as farm manager after they have qualified at agricultural college. Agricultural land, and therefore farms, are very expensive and the number of hands employed has been greatly reduced. In fact, because of the amount of machinery used, it is the mechanics who service this agricultural machinery who are more in demand.

However, there are other jobs that are linked with farming, such as veterinary surgeons and veterinary nurses, land agents, sales representatives for companies dealing in agricultural property and market inspectors.

There are also plenty of other jobs that are not office-bound. Sales representatives are out and about a great deal of the time – though often in their cars; so are members of the police, the armed services and the Merchant Navy. Jobs linked with the environment include local authority parks and recreational facility managers, market gardeners, foresters, horticulturalists, conservationists and landscape architects. Building and quantity surveyors spend time in wellies, too, visiting building sites, along with architects and other building and civil engineering experts. Nothing sounds more desk-bound than a bank manager, yet that can also be a job that entails making visits to customers, advising on small businesses and discussing loans.

Working out of doors, full time or some of the time, means being prepared to go out in cold, wet weather and on early winter mornings, as well as in summer sunshine. There are days when a warm office has its benefits!

3. School Subjects ...
Where Do You Shine?

The fact that you do not necessarily need A level mathematics to train in accountancy, but do need GCSE English language or equivalent as an engineer (to be able to write intelligible reports) demonstrates that aptitude in school subjects does not point the way directly towards a choice of career – but, of course, the ones you are good at do provide some guidelines.

MATHS AND SCIENCES

Personnel managers looking for people to work in their engineering departments would urge anyone who is reasonably proficient at maths and physics (including girls) not to drop these subjects too early but to continue with them for as long as possible to give themselves the chance to go into engineering, which is a career that is much in demand. This includes the main branches of engineering (electrical, electronic and mechanical) at all levels – professional, technician and draughtsman/woman.

There are some careers that particularly require maths, such as (obviously) economist, which covers all kinds of subjects, from agriculture to history; statisticians cover the same wide range in industrial, scientific or academic research and in working for the government's statistical service. Operational research departments need mathematicians to help with organisational and planning problems in various types of organisation such as airports, where the operational research group is responsible for planning the flow of passengers, and baggage and traffic movements to cause the least hiatus possible. In industry, mathematicians may work as one of a team in research, engineering, systems engineering and real-time programming connected with avionics, telecommunications and other fast-moving industries. Being at least numerate is a requirement for many types of industrial and commercial work.

Maths is also needed for careers such as air traffic control officers and assistants (high-pressure work; difficult to get into), and, naturally, careers in the financial world of banking, building societies and insurance, including clerks as well as accountants and finance directors. Other careers using maths (though sometimes a science is accepted as an alternative) are architecture and various types of surveying and civil engineering, both at professional and at technician assistant level.

Most of the science-based careers will require maths as well as the relevant science. These include all the various branches of medicine, dentistry, nursing and veterinary surgery, and the research jobs connected with them; also, of course, any type of scientific job including biochemist, chemical engineer, industrial physicist, food scientist and technologist, fuel and energy technologist, biological scientist (working in the food industry, or in research in improving crops or drugs), industrial chemist, scientific officer in the Civil Service, pharmacist and laboratory technician, materials scientist (working in industry on materials such as metals and alloys, ceramics, polymers, glass, paints and varnishes, inorganic chemicals), ceramics or glass technologist, geologist and geophysicist (study of the earth and atmosphere).

Maths and physics would also be necessary if you were intending to be an astronomer – but that is not the kind of profession for which there is a great demand, something you should always check before embarking on a course of study for a particular career.

There are many other careers where maths and sciences are not vital, but useful. Among them are jobs in computing: data processor, computer programmer and systems analyst; also production engineer, company secretary, buyer or purchaser and other management jobs. Generally, a maths and science base is very useful for a large variety of careers, although the subjects may not be put to direct use; this is partly because of the growing use of computers and statistical analysis, and partly because a qualification in maths gives an employer a guide to a candidate's ability.

Teaching and lecturing are obvious possible careers for any school-taught subject, and because industry has attracted so many maths and science graduates, there is now a shortage of teachers in these subjects, needed to help train the next generation of industrial technocrats.

Normally, jobs that require physics need maths as well, and those that require biology usually need chemistry, so physics and biology are not likely to be subjects that would go together. It is an advantage to have decided what kind of career is likely to suit you before giving up a science subject so that you can check on which qualifications will be needed – and if you want to keep up with all of them, and have a scientific bent, so much the better. There are also many jobs for which you would need qualifications in all three – physics, maths and chemistry.

Of course, as we saw earlier, maths and sciences are very marketable qualifications, especially at graduate level, for good jobs in commercial and industrial management.

ARTS AND LANGUAGES

It is often suggested that girls are more likely to be guided towards arts subjects (including history and literature) at school, than towards the sciences and maths. They should resist this attitude unless they really do prefer arts subjects.

Arts subjects at university are those other than science, medicine, theology and economics. With the growth of the leisure and entertainment sector and information services, arts-based skills will become more in demand, and there are some careers that will compare in status – and salary – with those in industry and finance, for instance in advertising and law.

On the artistically creative side, there are an awful lot of art-school students who will find it difficult to get the kind of jobs they want at the end of their course. Newly qualified painters or sculptors will have to subsidise their work by teaching, or begin in commercial work until they can afford to go it alone (working in a field such as advertising is a good way of learning to be business-like). Students who choose subjects such as graphic design will be able to work in a wide variety of fields: page layout design for magazines, brochures, advertisements, book jackets, record sleeves, etc; computer graphics takes you into the world of video and television; industrial design includes not only the packaging of products, but also the products themselves.

With constantly changing street fashions, young designers do have the chance of making a go of their career, and perhaps of running their own small business. Others may find a market for their ideas in Europe and choose to move abroad.

Other careers that can follow art-school training include photography (including medical photography), interior design, jewellery and silver design, the making of hand-crafted products, window dressing and display work. Architects, landscape architects, architectural technicians and draughtsmen/women, occupational therapists and beauticians are also in careers suitable for those who are good at art.

An obvious career for someone who is good at languages would seem to be as a translator or interpreter, but interpreting, especially, needs a very high standard indeed; it is necessary to be bilingual as well as being able to cope with a very demanding method of working. There are not a great number of jobs either in interpreting or translating (which usually means translating written work). Languages are more useful as an adjunct to other qualifications, for instance in jobs that involve marketing products overseas, and the single market gives increased importance to European languages. There are many university courses that combine languages with other subjects such as science or engineering. There are also courses for diplomas in languages and secretarial studies, languages for business, and languages and marketing. The tourist industry calls for the use of foreign languages, and although European languages are obviously useful, being able to speak Arabic, Japanese, Cantonese or one of the languages which are not taught in schools, but whose countries increasingly have trade or tourism links with the UK, is a great advantage.

The 'arts' subjects, such as history, can be taken up to postgraduate level and then used, perhaps combined with a business or computer studies course, in an industrial or commercial management job or in something based on writing, such as journalism, advertising copywriting, or public and press relations work. Other careers that can follow on from 'arts' subjects include barrister, solicitor and other types of work associated with the legal profession, and careers in the armed services, the Civil Service and local government.

Teaching (language, science and maths teachers are in demand), secretarial work, retailing, and the interesting but not numerous openings in museum work, archivist, information science, librarianship and patent work are other 'arts' possibilities.

The AS levels allow for more subjects to be studied in the sixth form, so that those who are good at languages as well as science will not have to drop a useful foreign language, for instance, to concentrate exclusively on the science subjects. It is also possible to broaden areas of study with complementary AS levels, so that science can be taken along with design and technology. Universities, and many large companies and professional bodies, count two AS levels as one A level pass.

Don't give up a subject that you are good at and enjoy if it could give you the A level grade you need to get into university.

PRACTICAL APTITUDE

If you are good at needlework or crochet, how about a career in electronics? If you have ever noticed the tangle of wires underneath a telephone cable inspection hatch you will see why that is a serious suggestion. There are many kinds of work that require dexterity of this kind: dentistry, jewellery craftwork, radio officer (Merchant Navy), carpentry, surgery, laboratory work, as well as electrical and mechanical engineers and, of course, work connected with the making of clothes, hats and wigs.

Anyone who is good at mending engines or electrical equipment and enjoys school classes in woodwork and metalwork should consider careers in the various types of engineering, either at professional or technician and craft levels.

Careers that involve practical aptitude can be the ones that give you more freedom and chance to use your imagination than a great deal of office work: for instance, horticulture, camera operator, chef or cook, model-making (for exhibitions etc), furniture design, musical instrument making, shopfitting, floristry, occupational therapy, specialist building work, upholstery and even, if you are fit enough, blacksmithing.

SPORT

Unfortunately, being captain of all the school sports teams does not guarantee a career as a football or tennis star – that happens only to the very few – or even a career as a PE teacher. There are other qualities that are needed besides – to be a star (in anything) requires determination and luck, and a certain amount of talent. To be a PE teacher it is necessary to do the normal teacher training course of three to four years, with the entry requirements of two or three A level passes and up to three GCSE passes at grade C or above, including maths and English language and PGCE (Postgraduate Certificate of Education) in physical education or a BEd in physical education.

There are degree, DipHE, HND and postgraduate courses at universities and other colleges in sports studies, including sport and recreation studies and sports science.

A levels in sports studies and PE are now available at schools and colleges; for details of the syllabus contact the Associated Examining Board, Stag Hill House, Guildford, Surrey GU2 5XJ. The sports studies course is academic and concentrates on the technical analysis of sport, combining elements of sociology, psychology, medicine and science; entrants will not need to be good at sport themselves. The PE course is similar but does include assessment of physical activities. The A levels should be of value to those who want to go into the sport and leisure industry.

Sport as a leisure-time activity can provide work for proficient sports men and women who have the right training. It is possible to qualify for coaching while doing a degree in sports studies, a teaching course or studying for a diploma in youth and community work. Opportunities include posts as swimming teachers, golf club professionals, local authority sports centre coaches in various sports, mountain leaders and sports leaders at holiday centres – holiday camps, ski and outdoor pursuit centres, private hotels and leisure centres. The leisure and fitness industry provides plenty of opportunities. Sportswear and sports-based publicity can also provide spin-off work. There are also physical training instructors taken on by the armed services – they must be aged 17, and competition for places is strong.

For a list of training and educational courses in sport and recreation, including universities offering sports scholarships, and information about careers, contact the Sports Council Information Centre, enclosing £2.50 to cover postage and packing.

Other careers based on physical activities are attached to the medical services, such as physiotherapy.

4. You as a Person ...
Your Likes, Dislikes and Talents

Certain jobs that you may be very well suited to academically may not appeal to you on other grounds; there is no point in applying to be a scaffolder if you are afraid of heights – or in studying to be an architect, either. If you are afraid of flying, you will not be among the large number of people whose ambition is to be an air stewardess. So it is important to weigh up the non-academic pros and cons when considering a career.

DO YOU GET ON WELL WITH PEOPLE?

Working as an air stewardess or steward is in reality more to do with looking after people than with travel. Applicants may have heady visions of visits to exotic places, but air crews are more likely to spend rest days abroad beside a standard hotel pool than sightseeing, or work as waiters and waitresses of the air on short hops between London and Brussels and back. But if they like people – meeting them, caring for them, helping them when they are in difficulties or apprehensive, this is fulfilling work, with some excitement thrown in, and the status of wearing a uniform.

Jobs involving people break down into different categories. There are the ones caring for the sick and needy, others that mean meeting the public, perhaps selling products and services to them.

Caring jobs, of course, are based particularly within the medical services – not only doctors, dentists and nurses, but those out in the community as well: health visitors, social workers and welfare officers. Such work calls for a real commitment to the people concerned, who may be very young or old, tragically sick, dirty or confused. Community services such as the police, fire and ambulance services call for the same caring attitude in certain circumstances, too. There are also private organisations involved in care work, including the NSPCC and other aid agencies, nursing homes, and nursery schools and playgroups for young children.

There are some types of work that do not immediately seem to involve a caring attitude, but sympathy and understanding may often be needed by clients or customers. Solicitors, for example, will often be dealing with problems of a personal nature, as will accountants, insurance claims officers, housing officers and even veterinary surgeons, who often find they are treating a distressed pet owner as much as the pet itself.

People who work in the 'personal services' jobs, such as hairdressing, beauty therapy, and many areas of the tourism and leisure industries, must enjoy meeting people, give them willing and cheerful service, and sometimes be able to cope with minor emergencies – such as the irate people in the queue at the check-in desk who learn that their flight will be hours late.

Being behind the shop counter as assistant or manager (or owner) brings you into contact with large numbers of people and demands another type of skill: being able to sell to them. If you have ever helped out in the local paper shop or at a jumble sale, or asked people to sponsor you for some charitable activity, you will know something about it: persuading people to buy things is one skill that can take you right up to a top marketing position within a large organisation selling either manufactured products, or services, such as insurance.

Being able to get on well with people is a great help not only in the caring, personal services and selling jobs, but in any situation where you are one of a group. In any office or factory you will need to be able to cope with difficult colleagues and make positive relationships; in engineering work, for example, you will need to be able to fit in as a member of a team.

COULD YOU WORK ON YOUR OWN?

Very few people work entirely on their own, unless they work from home. But jobs that mean travelling long distances alone, as sales representatives do, or being the only person doing a particular type of job in a large organisation, such as a receptionist, can give rise to feelings of isolation. In a different way, being in charge of a department, or your own business, means that you have sole responsibility for important decisions and this can sometimes set you apart from others around you.

Working overseas, for instance on a VSO scheme or as a team manager, can mean that you wind up as the only European for miles around, and it is not easy to cope with isolation of this kind. This situation does not happen often and aid agencies, in particular, try to avoid it – but it is worth checking out when you are thinking of a post overseas.

DO YOU LIKE RESPONSIBILITY?

If your school activities have included running the chess or photography club, being games captain, a member of the school council or prefect, an employer or personnel officer will be pleased to hear it. It is not just the armed services who are looking for 'leadership material' but employers recruiting engineering apprentices, management staff, and even research scientists who will need to be able to direct the team of scientists and laboratory technicians working with them.

Employers also look for people who can work as team members and the nature of some project work may change so that more decisions are taken by the whole group and not by one manager. The best manager will be a team leader who is willing to co-operate with the other members of the team to bring about a result.

Membership of any group that involves out-of-school activities, such as games and PE clubs, drama clubs, choirs and orchestras, cadet corps, Scouts and Guides, will prove to an employer (or college interviewer) that you have interests beyond the television screen. Part-time jobs are a plus in their estimation, too: delivering newspapers, serving in a shop, washing up or waiting in a restaurant and so forth demonstrate that you have the entrepreneurial spirit and are not afraid of work. Jobs of that kind also prove that you can get up early in the mornings (newspaper delivery), can accept working in a hot and steamy atmosphere (kitchen assistant), and can get on well with the public (shop assistant).

SPARE-TIME INTERESTS

Activities that you enjoy doing outside school may point the way to a career – if you enjoy taking engines apart and putting them back together again (successfully), then obviously you should consider the idea of being a mechanic or professional mechanical engineer. If you are good at carpentry, a City and Guilds course in carpentry and joinery, or in furniture design or design craft could lead to you setting up your own business.

Knitting has been a profitable pastime recently; as long as the garments also have designer flair, sewing or knitting, combined with artistic ability, could take you into a career, after an art-school course, that could lead to a home-based small business, in upholstery or millinery as well as garments. There is also the possibility of working in the wardrobe department at a theatre, film or television company.

Archaeology is a fascinating spare-time interest and there are university courses in the subject – but not a lot of jobs at the end of the day. However, a degree could lead to a related job as museum curator – and anyway, a degree is no bad thing. It is a qualification you can use towards other types of work, so study of a subject of this kind that gives real pleasure would certainly not be a waste of time, even if the subject remains only a lifetime's hobby.

Another interest that may continue as a fulfilling hobby, or be turned into a career, is music. Those who aspire to be millionaire pop stars will probably know enough about the pop music industry to have realised that for every 'overnight success' (who has probably been struggling for years), there are many individuals and groups who never make it. A college-based training in music could not only be a useful first step on the road to fame, but would also be an advantage to those who become 'session' musicians, backing pop groups or recording for radio or television, and would allow some teaching, too.

Teaching, rather than performing, and music therapy are also possible careers for the classical musician. Only a very few top-flight musicians are able to sustain a career giving concerts and recitals, and places in professional orchestras and choirs are few and strongly competed for. Working as a professional musician also means very unsocial hours, hard work and low financial rewards. However, there are other jobs within related businesses: in recording, retailing, radio and television, music publishing and musical instrument technology (there is a demand, for instance, for handcrafted bows for stringed instruments).

ARE YOU KEEN ON SPORT?

Careers in sport were discussed in the previous chapter: if you are not suited to them, yet enjoy playing sports in your spare time, you should bear in mind that large commercial companies and organisations, such as the Civil Service and the armed services, offer facilities for various kinds of sport as leisure activities. There will usually be sports and social committees who take care of the organisation of facilities and events and there could be opportunities for football, cricket, netball, tennis, table tennis, badminton, swimming, and anything else for which there is a reasonable demand – maybe archery or fishing. Some companies have their own large sports grounds, so if you are very keen to carry on with the sports you followed at school or college, find out about sports facilities as part of your research on companies when applying for job interviews.

You can also keep up your sport by joining clubs, and by helping out with local youth groups, who may desperately need support.

ARE YOU SQUEAMISH?

A medical student's training sorts out the sheep from the goats very speedily – the first part of the course is devoted to the dissection of cadavers (dead bodies) which gives rise to some fairly horrific 'true' stories circulating among the students: did you hear the one about the chap who took a spare arm with him on the tube, and left it hanging from the strap when he got off? Not true, one hopes, but if you can't cope with that sort of humour (let alone the dissection) then a career in medicine is not for you.

Fainting at the sight of blood, vomit or worse is also no recommendation for a career in medicine, nursing, animal nursing or as a pathology laboratory technician. Laboratory technicians, too, would have to consider their position on the question of animals being used to test drugs.

There are a few other questions that you need to ask yourself when thinking about a career: whether you are willing to work in noisy conditions, for example (though not all factories are noisy); whether you would prefer to be working with people of your own sex; whether you could, and would like to, cope with people who are physically or mentally ill or handicapped; whether you would be prepared to take risks affecting your safety, speak in public, or be away from home for short or long periods.

COULD YOU COPE WITH SHIFT WORK OR UNSOCIAL HOURS?

Shift work (for which you must be aged 18 or over) is a way of life for people who work in airports, hospitals, the police, factories where the plant has to be kept going night and day, the armed services, the Merchant Navy and sectors of the tourist industry. It means alternating nights on duty with days on duty, and having time off when everyone else is at work.

Being an airline pilot, for instance, is a highly paid job, but it badly affects social life (rosters are often worked out only a few days in advance) and holidays, since these can only be taken at times of the year when bookings are down; pilots can be constantly tired, because even if they are not jet-lagged the chances are that they are doing night flights and disrupting their normal sleep pattern. (It is also, one pilot said, no great fun to be sitting in the middle of a thunderstorm in the middle of the night, terrified out of your wits.) At other times it can be boring work; the long-haul flights in particular can get very tedious, as can the repetition of short-haul flights.

People who work in shops, restaurants and the entertainment business must be prepared for unsocial hours, which means rarely being able to see friends during their leisure time – so many people may find themselves making friends more among their colleagues than outside their working life.

HEALTH AND PHYSIQUE

There are many types of work that need physical stamina: not only those to do with agriculture, forestry, sport and the construction industry, but out-and-about jobs such as veterinary work (which can also involve long hours on duty), surveying, police work, medicine and nursing (constant physical, mental and emotional strain, plus long hours on the feet and on duty), and various activities in the armed services. Some work involves standing for long periods (hairdressing), or working in an awkward or cramped position (dentistry, jewellery-making). So if you know that your physical stamina is not good, there is no point in aiming for a career that you know you will not be able to cope with.

In some types of work there are restrictions on height, for instance air cabin crews (minimum 5 ft 2 in [158 cm] to 6 ft 2 in [188 cm] and weight must be in proportion! – partly dictated by the cabin height and positioning of luggage racks).

There are other health factors that may also have an effect on the type of work you can do. One of the most important is bad colour vision which immediately cancels out careers such as pilot, air traffic controller, electronics engineer, radio officer and laboratory technician. Good eyesight is also often required; again, it is worth checking. Other factors that may also need to be taken into account are skin allergies, such as eczema and dermatitis, that can affect your ability to work with chemicals in industry, in a photographer's darkroom, in catering or in hairdressing, or if they arise from contact with animals, would prevent you working in a vet's surgery or in the fur trade. Asthma could also be a problem, especially in a job that involves work in a dusty, stuffy or fume-laden atmosphere. Other factors are diabetes, migraine and epilepsy – and if you suffer from defective hearing, you will not, presumably, think of becoming an acoustics engineer.

Students who have any kind of disability can contact Skill, the National Bureau for Students with Disabilities, 336 Brixton Road, London SW9 7AA or the Royal Association for Disability and Rehabilitation (RADAR) at Unit 12, City Forum, 250 City Road, London EC1V 8AF. If you are disabled, aged between 18–30 and want to set up your own business, the Prince's Youth Business Trust offers loans, a grant of up to £1500 and the services of a business adviser. The address is 18 Park Square East, London NW1 4LH.

COULD YOU COPE WITH A LONG PERIOD OF STUDY?

University courses leading to a first degree last from three to four years, and a full doctor's, dentist's or veterinary surgeon's training is even longer. Postgraduate courses can add up to three years' extra study, and further study for entry to professional bodies can spin out study time still more. Therefore it is important to be working towards something you really want to do, or on a subject that you enjoy, to find the motivation to work on your own, cope with life away from home and achieve good results. Having gained a place at university at all means that you should be capable of managing academically, but if getting the relevant A level results was more of a miserable strain than a happy achievement – or if you have not got to that stage yet, but are justifiably apprehensive – perhaps you should consider approaching the job you may have in mind from another angle. Your head teacher or sixth form tutor will be able to advise you.

5. Women and a Career

Because the majority of women do have babies – though others choose not to – their career patterns have to be different from those of men. While a man is able to continue progressing smoothly up the ladder, gaining promotions and jumps in salary, a woman who wants a family has to break her career, either for a few weeks, or for several years, just at the time when her career may be beginning to take off. Nearly all women (around 90 per cent) will return to work eventually, for both financial and other reasons, so those who intend to continue using their abilities to the full must give careful thought at the outset to planning their careers.

Some women, particularly the committed and highly qualified professional ones, take only a few weeks off when they have a baby and return to full-time work as soon as possible. Under the Employment Protection Act women are entitled to reinstatement for up to 29 weeks after the birth – provided they have told the employer in writing and before taking maternity leave that they wish to return, and provided they have worked for the same company for at least two years full time, or five years part time, up to 11 weeks before the baby is due. Under EC law all pregnant workers are entitled to 14 weeks' continuous leave, which can be taken before or after childbirth. Professional women will probably employ a nanny or child-minder when they return to work (for which they receive no tax relief, although their employers may be willing to employ the child-minder themselves and so help overcome that hurdle). If they add to their family later, they will do the same with each child so that they can continue their career. Some women, of course, may be able to hand over their babies to the care of their mothers during the working day – but it is likely that their mothers would prefer to be working themselves!

Often the women who go back to work full time switch over to part-time working later, perhaps because they find combining the running of both a home and a full-time job too much, but want to 'keep their hand in' with part-time work. Unfortunately, it has to be said that most working women with families do find running both a home and a job tiring and stressful. Husbands are inclined to think that they are doing more to help than they in fact are, although they probably agree in principle that their wives should be able to work if they want to. Prospective husbands should be questioned searchingly on whether they are prepared to be fully supportive should the need arise!

A problem for a woman going back to work on a part-time basis is that she may be forced to settle for a job with a lower status. One of the growth areas in jobs has been for women part-timers, but these have very often been badly paid jobs in the 'service industries'. Only able to work while their children are at school or their husbands or mothers are able to look after them, these women have worked in shops, cafés, pubs, restaurants and in cleaning jobs for low wages and often with none of the benefits of paid holidays, sick pay and occupational pension schemes available to those in full-time employment. Although crèches at the workplace are seen by some people as an ideal solution, there are still very few in the UK. Benefits such as maternity leave and pension rights may eventually become compulsory for part-timers under EC law. Job-sharing is another idea that is becoming more acceptable to employers and may be more widely established in the future.

The way to overcome as far as possible the disadvantages of the 'career break' is to aim for qualifications that will continue to be valued, or can be used constructively on a part-time basis. Although it sounds depressing, it should not be forgotten that many women do end up, for a variety of reasons, as single parents and as sole breadwinners, and so may need high earning capacity.

Both universities and employers are keen to attract girls into the careers where there are shortages of qualified graduates: in maths, science and engineering.

The Engineering Training Authority provides female students studying maths or physics A level (or equivalent) with the chance to find out whether an engineering career is for them. Students participating in the Insight Programme spend a week at one of ten universities around the country. Course subjects include contacts, practising engineers, information on education, training, careers and sponsorship; there is also a day in a local engineering company. Students pay a £25 registration fee but the course, which always has more applicants than places, is free. Contact the Engineering Training Authority on Freefone 0800 282167 and ask for an Insight Application pack. Alternatively, their address is 41 Clarendon Road, Watford, Herts WD1 1HS.

Female students should also contact Women into Science and Engineering, who are part of the Environmental Council.

As noted in previous chapters, electronic, electrical and mechanical engineering, and computer sciences, are fields in which there may be more job vacancies than qualified staff available. Engineering is an area that is still fairly new to women, but there are qualified women working in it at all levels: professional, technician and craft levels. They are becoming more commonplace and accepted on the factory floor and in senior positions. However, in some of the engineering disciplines – electronics, for example – technology is moving so fast that it could be difficult to return to a full-time job after a long break raising a family, although there are university courses which aim to plug the knowledge gap for women graduates in this situation. In other disciplines it would be possible to keep up to date by reading technical magazines and attending conferences and lectures, and then return.

Computer sciences could be a very valuable qualification, leading into consultancy work, and to working from home. Accountancy is useful for the same reason – there are always local businesses needing an accountant. Although women barristers find the going rather tough because they have to rely on others, in an extremely conservative profession, to give them work, women solicitors can continue working after a career break. There are refresher courses for them and they are able to keep up with developments by reading the appropriate literature.

There are four organisations, Women in Management, Women into Computing, Women in Banking and Finance and Women in the Public Sector Network, that have been formed to help women in these fields, partly through providing a network of useful contacts, such as men have, and partly by giving help and advice. Some aspects of management are very familiar to women: personnel and public relations, for instance; in others they are still making headway. They can find it difficult to get beyond middle management and into senior positions, but this is often because they are not assertive enough in letting their employers know that they want to make management their permanent career. Women who are successful would advise those who want to get on to take every opportunity for further training – press for it if necessary – and to be prepared to move around the country, when necessary, to gain experience. This need for mobility can cause problems for both husbands and wives, and both may prefer to stay at a lower level rather than force their spouse into a move that could harm a developing career. This problem can be overcome if one spouse works on a freelance basis and so can operate from anywhere.

Returning to work in management is not necessarily easy, especially if there are plenty of young newly qualified (and cheaper) applicants available for the work. When planning a career it makes sense to go for an area in which there are likely to be shortages, or train in a skill that is in great demand – one woman who had taken a seven-year break to raise a family took a PhD course in artificial intelligence, a science then only about three years old, and found herself getting excellent job offers because there were so few people in the UK with her training.

Training in any field that is new and growing should lead not only to more certainty of being able to return later, but also to more equality of opportunity – it is in the more established professions that old attitudes still linger.

Women who have an ambition to work abroad could also run into problems, especially in the Muslim countries where it would not be considered correct for a woman to be working with men – this can affect women with engineering and surveying qualifications. However, although veterinary surgeons, for instance, would not be able to do field work, they would be able to work 'behind the scenes' in laboratories, with other scientists.

Women are generally considered to be 'good with people' and have a tradition of working in medical support jobs, such as nursing, health visiting, physiotherapy, in personnel management and market research. Those who would want to return to a career in personnel management would have to keep up to date with changes in legislation in the meantime; it is a career that has changed a great deal in concept over the years. Many women are able to return to careers in the National Health Service or in the private medical sector. Dentistry, for instance, is considered to be the best of the professions for those wanting to return, and there are refresher courses to help them. Ruth Miller's book *Equal Opportunities* evaluates prospects for women 'returners' within each career.

Under the Sex Discrimination Act training can be provided for women who want to return to work, and they should ask for it to be made available to them. They can also undertake training on their own initiative, at a further education centre, through the Open University or on a TEC training scheme. A problem with part-time work is that it can be difficult to get on to employers' training schemes, and it may be necessary to be firm in convincing an employer that it would be worthwhile.

The teaching profession, of course, has always been looked upon as a classic way of allowing mothers to tie in their work with their children's needs. It is not as easy now for teachers to find full-time work in the area where they live, and they will also find themselves trapped at the bottom of the pay scale. However, many mothers are able to work as supply teachers, or on a part-time basis. Those most in demand are maths and science teachers (for those who have the relevant degrees it could be worth doing a teacher training course) and language teachers. Qualified musicians, too, can teach in schools and take private pupils at home.

In both professional and non-professional work, it is important to gain as many qualifications and as much experience as possible, whether you are doing this before starting a family, or as the basis for a permanent career. Some women will advise you to steer clear of the typewriter if you want to get ahead, otherwise you may remain chained to it (or a word processor) in an unsatisfying job. You will need to be fairly assertive in order to convince superiors that you really are keen on promotion, and must take every chance there is of further training. It has been noted that there often are better conditions, better pay and better promotion prospects in jobs where both men and women are working together; and there is more chance of promotion, too, in small firms rather than large ones.

In the armed services, women now have the opportunity to train in technical subjects, with the same career opportunities.

Banking also allows women to move up into top positions – more so than in some other careers, such as insurance.

Women whose work is valued by their employers are often contacted by them, and asked to return after starting a family; others may take on entirely different types of work, found through their personal network of friends or relations. An increasing number use the business skills they have previously gained to start their own small businesses – anything from selling double glazing to running transport hire firms or franchise clothes shops. Over the past decade the number of women running their own businesses has almost trebled – more women than men enter self-employment and three out of ten new businesses are now started by women. Being your own boss is a sure way to beat discrimination!

Part 3

6. *Training*

If you have decided what type of work appeals to you, and have identified a goal to aim for, your next decision will be whether to continue in full-time higher education by going on to take a course at a college, or whether to apply to join a company's training scheme that will give you the qualifications and experience you need.

Those who are still undecided should continue with full-time education, if possible. Concentrate on subjects that are always marketable (especially maths and sciences) if you know you will be able to do well at them, or on subjects that will allow freedom of choice later – biology, for instance, is not as flexible as physics.

If your star subject is history, or English literature, you can continue it right up to degree level, and then convert it into a useful qualification for a career such as accountancy, teaching, management, law or computer programming. You may do a postgraduate course, and decide only during that year of study what your final theatre of operations will be.

Getting a place on a degree course is by no means easy, and there are often major disappointments when the A level results arrive. They may call for a re-think of strategy, but not a leap in the dark into a course that you would not enjoy. Alternatives include a BTEC HND/HNC course at a university or college of higher education, or A level entry to an organisation such as the Civil Service, a large company, banking or insurance where there are training schemes combined with practical experience.

FULL-TIME EDUCATION

Degree courses
There are certain degree courses that are 'vocational' and lead straight into a career, such as medicine, architecture, surveying, veterinary science, accountancy, dentistry, engineering and law. Others may seem vocational, such as sociology or psychology, but will not necessarily lead to work with the social services or

National Health Service and, like zoology and philosophy, are not particularly sought after in the job market, except as evidence that you have been able successfully to complete a degree course. There is a very wide range of courses on offer at universities, but it is up to you to decide which ones will enable you to combine enjoyment of the subject with positive value in career terms.

Minimum entry requirement for a degree course is three GCSE passes and two at A level or H Grade SCE in Scotland (GCSE and A level or H Grade SCE passed in the same subject are not counted as two, and in some cases two attempts at a pass are also unacceptable). Combinations of AS and A levels, and BTEC National Certificates and Diplomas are also acceptable. Some subjects, such as medicine, veterinary science and pharmacology, require three subjects with high grades. Competition for degree places, especially in popular subjects such as medicine and law, is fierce, and having the correct grades does not guarantee entry to every course. On the other hand, courses in engineering and the manufacturing industries are often undersubscribed, with the result that some universities will offer engineering degree courses to applicants who do not have the relevant science A levels, and there is a possibility that A level physics will be dropped altogether as a requirement for an engineering course – though maths will still be necessary. There are also conversion courses for those who do not have the right qualifications.

Although not all candidates are interviewed for places, even in medical or veterinary schools, interviews can be crucial in the granting of places, and so must be taken very seriously by the candidate. (Prospective art students need to have built up a good portfolio of their work to take along to interviews, if they are trying for a practical arts course.)

As well as demanding GCSE and A level passes or H Grade SCE passes in certain subjects for each degree course, the universities also have general entrance requirements; in addition, being able to offer a broad base of GCSE subjects and an extra A/AS level or H Grade SCE, if possible, will be of more use than having only the minimum required. The *UCAS Handbook*, published by the Universities and Colleges Admissions Service (free) lists full-time or sandwich first degree, DipHE and HND courses; *University and College Entrance: The Official Guide* from Sheed and Ward Ltd, 14 Coopers Row, London EC3N 2BH, price £12 plus £3 p&p, lists courses and entry requirements; they should both be available from your school careers teacher or library. CRAC produce a wide range of publications concerned with many aspects of education and training, including NVQs, GNVQs and modern apprenticeships. The universities' individual entry requirements can be checked from their own prospectuses, which they will send you free of charge. Some of the prospectuses are very well produced and informative about the courses and university life; others, perhaps from universities that do not need to attract students, are more basic. Write to the registrar of several universities for their prospectuses so that you get a good overall picture. Again, your local careers office should have copies.

Choosing which universities to apply for entails quite a bit of research – first, into your own abilities. There is no point in aiming for a university whose entry requirements are beyond you, so you should have full and frank discussions with your teachers about your capabilities; they will be able to assess pretty accurately what grades you will be likely to achieve. It is then important to look in great detail at the courses being offered; they do not cover the same ground in every university and it is possible to find yourself on a course whose content differs from what you really wanted. You can write to the admissions tutors of the courses you are considering for further information and advice.

The next part of your homework – and this is more difficult – concerns the quality of the courses. Talking to people who were at university some years ago may not help you; they may subconsciously be loyal to their own place of learning, and teaching staff may have changed. An off-the-record chat to a careers officer or schools liaison officer from a professional institute or from the kind of large company that you are eventually aiming for could give you a clearer picture.

As you probably know, there are differences between the types of universities. The oldest, most academic and most prestigious are Oxford and Cambridge. (The oldest in Scotland is St Andrews.) You are normally expected to apply directly to the college of your choice for a place, rather than to the university, and application must be made earlier than in the case of other universities – by 15 October. The younger 'red brick' universities grew up in or near large cities, for example London, Birmingham, Bristol, Hull, Manchester, Southampton and Stirling, and offer a wide variety of degree courses. The 'technological' universities, such as Aston, Bath, Brunel, Loughborough, Salford and Strathclyde, have an established tradition of applied science and engineering degrees, sometimes based on 'sandwich' courses (see below), and have also recently diversified into courses in the humanities and social sciences. The sixties-built 'new' campus universities are often outside the nearest town; they include York, East Anglia, Sussex, Warwick and Lancaster.

Many universities offer practical experience which is contained in a 'sandwich' course, thus combining academic teaching with on-the-job training. The courses may be college-based or work-based and sponsored by an employer. A sponsored student will be paid by the employer for the time that is spent working and there is no need for the college or student to find suitable places for the work experience. Sandwich courses are normally longer than college-based courses – four years instead of three (or four in Scotland). A 'thick' sandwich usually takes the form of two years spent in college, one year with an employer and a final year at college. A 'thin' sandwich divides the first three years between college and employer for equal periods, with the final year spent in college. Sandwich courses apply not only to technical courses but also to courses in law, business studies, economics and many others. They can be very successful in leading to jobs.

There is, of course, competition for sponsorships, and it is best to apply to employers as early as possible – at least 12 months before the start of the course. Those interested in engineering should write to the Engineering Council, the Engineering Training Authority or one of the numerous bodies that administer information services about the trade and ask them for a publications list. These booklets are usually invaluable and some, such as *Engineering Opportunities* from the Schools Liaison Service of the Institution of Mechanical Engineers, provide details of sponsorship and training.

Another useful book is *Sponsorships for Students*, published by Biblios, Star Road, Partridge Green, West Sussex RH13 8LD; telephone 01403 710971 (£7.95 + p&p).

In addition there is the Open University which provides study through correspondence course backed up by local study centres and radio and television programmes. There are no formal entry requirements needed, except that students must be aged 21 or over. University College, Buckingham is an independent university; it offers a small range of specialist degrees, but its fees are not totally covered by local education authority grants.

The final piece of research is very important; you will be spending three or four years at a university so it is necessary to consider what else, other than academically, you hope to get out of it. Study the facilities within the university and surrounding area. For a country-lover who likes the fresh air and wants to go climbing every weekend, the last place to go would be London. On the other hand, if you want to experience big city life, somewhere like London, Manchester or Leeds is a more obvious choice. Accommodation should also be taken into account: being in a hall of residence can be an important part of the learning process, and helpful to those living away from home for the first time, but such a place is almost non-existent in, for instance, London.

As well as degree courses, universities and colleges of higher education provide training for a number of other qualifications. They include foundation courses, which require A level entry, and lead on to further courses in subjects such as art and design, accountancy and engineering. (More information about art and design courses is given in *Design Courses in Britain*, published by Trotman and Co, 12 Hill Rise, Richmond, Surrey TW10 6UA (£11.50) and in the UCAS *Handbook*, published by the Universities and Colleges Admissions Service – free.) There are also professional courses which lead to, or provide exemption from, examinations of some of the professional institutions; more information about these can be obtained from the professional institutions concerned. It is important to check before applying for these professional courses that you would be eligible for an LEA grant, as this is not always the case.

Other courses available are BTEC/SCOTVEC National Certificate and Diploma (NC and ND) and BTEC/SCOTVEC Higher National Certificate and Diploma (HNC and HND). These certificates and diplomas are awarded in a wide range of subjects based on technical, scientific, business and design studies, and are primarily intended to lead to work in industry and commerce. These programmes may be based on full-time, block-release or sandwich format, or may use a combination of these study methods (block release means that you are employed, but are released for unbroken periods of five or six weeks or more in order to study).

Entry requirements to the lower level National Certificate and Diploma courses vary, normally four GCSE passes, BTEC First or equivalent, and are considered to be at around A level standard. They can lead into Higher National Certificate and Diploma courses. These HNC and HND courses normally require qualifications of at least one A level or equivalent, or BTEC National qualifications. The Higher Diploma is considered to be just below degree standard and is a widely accepted qualification; it can also be used for entry to continued study to degree level at the same college, or at a different institution.

Another qualification is the DipHE (Diploma of Higher Education). The course, lasting two years, can be built up from various options and components and can lead into either a BEd (Bachelor of Education) or other degree course, but the composition of the course must be chosen carefully, otherwise it may not be possible to transfer. It is usefully flexible for those who have not decided on a career, but is not normally used as a qualification for getting a job.

Other colleges

There are also colleges of higher education (many of which fulfil their original function as teacher training institutions), colleges of further education, colleges of technology, technical colleges, colleges of commerce, colleges of art, and horticultural and agricultural colleges, all of which offer a range of courses which may include degrees and perhaps postgraduate qualifications.

As an example of the courses offered, one college of technology offers BTEC Diploma courses in business studies, engineering, building studies, civil engineering studies, science, computer studies, hotel, catering and institutional operations, and HNC or HND courses in computer-aided engineering, electronic engineering and computer technology, computer technology (real-time programming), electronics and communications engineering, production engineering and applied biology.

At some of these colleges it is possible to re-take GCSE/A level exams, or to take extra subjects, and to take City and Guilds of London Institute (CGLI) examinations (see page 101).

There are also independent colleges specialising in a range of subjects. The Council for the Accreditation of Correspondence Colleges monitors standards for independent colleges.

Further reading for more detailed information on college courses and higher education: *British Qualifications: a comprehensive guide to educational, technical, professional and academic qualifications in Britain* (Kogan Page); *It's Your Choice* (book and video) from the Department for Education and Employment Publications Centre, PO Box 2193, London E15 2EU.

COURSES IN ART AND DESIGN

Applications to art and design courses previously made through the Art and Design Admissions Registry (ADAR), are now made through UCAS. This change takes effect from the 1997 academic year. Applicants for courses have up to six choices.

Most applicants will first have completed a Foundation course in art and design, or a BTEC National Diploma in general art and design, though a very few may enter college straight from school.

COURSES IN TEACHER TRAINING

Application for teacher training courses, including Art Teacher's Certificate/Diploma courses, is through the UCAS scheme. Applicants for teacher posts in all maintained and grant-maintained schools, as well as in many private schools, must hold qualified teacher status (QTS). *The NATFHE Handbook of Initial Teacher Training* lists courses of teacher education at both undergraduate and postgraduate levels, including details of courses that normally lead to QTS award; £12 from Linneys ESL, Newgate Lane, Mansfield, Notts NG18 2PA.

CITY AND GUILDS (CGLI)

The City and Guilds examinations are the ones for crafts, and can be taken in schools, local colleges, training centres, and by members of the armed services and the Merchant Navy. They cover many subjects, including bakery, carpentry, dental technician, horticulture, motor mechanic, painting and decorating, hairdressing and tailoring. There is a full list of subjects in the COIC annual guide to opportunities and trends in employment, *Occupations*.

CERTIFICATE OF PRE-VOCATIONAL EDUCATION (CPVE)

The Certificate of Pre-vocational Education is designed to give students with a few GCSEs practical experience in the workings of business industry, a chance to study a range of job-related topics, and the opportunity to improve general skills in such areas as using figures and using computers. The certificate is proof of completion of the course – not a pass. The course is available in some schools and colleges of further education.

NATIONAL VOCATIONAL QUALIFICATIONS (NVQs)

National Vocational Qualifications are assessed in a work

situation, either at college or in a job. They have study units, some based on practical skills and others based on written work, with a range of requirements. Different units can be built up to a complete NVQ. Most colleges offer NVQ courses, and the qualifications are designed to give employers an idea of a job candidate's capabilities, both in the UK and, eventually, throughout the EU. Many organisations such as City and Guilds, BTEC and RSA offer qualifications which are also NVQs.

The qualifications cover a range of jobs and careers, including agriculture, horticulture, engineering, construction, manufacturing, catering, hairdressing, retailing, sport and recreation, caring, environmental conservation, information technology, management, publishing, journalism and language. There is a range of five levels, from Level 1, which is straightforward tasks and skills, to Level 5, which requires high-level managerial responsibilities. In engineering, Levels 1 and 2 are awarded for standards associated with jobs at operator level; Level 3 is the recognised qualification for those at Engineering Technician and Craft level; Level 4 is for those at Incorporated Engineer level and Level 5 awards are being developed for those at professional engineer level.

NVQs do not apply in Scotland, where similar qualifications are known as SVQs.

GENERAL NATIONAL VOCATIONAL QUALIFICATIONS (GNVQs)

GNVQs are designed to offer students a broadly based qualification which is something of a cross between academic and vocational training programmes. The courses are normally full time and offered at three levels: Foundation, Intermediate and Advanced. Whereas the NVQ qualifications prepare you for a specific job, the GNVQs allow you to keep your options open, preparing you instead for a range of jobs. Intermediate level is roughly equivalent to four GCSEs at grades A to C and are available in Art and Design, Business, Construction and Built Environment, Engineering, Health and Social Care, Hospitality and Catering, Information Technology, Leisure and Tourism, Manufacturing, Science, Retail and Distributive Services and Media. Foundation GNVQs are the equivalent of four GCSEs, grades D to G and are available in all of the above subjects apart from Retail and Distributive Services and Media.

ROYAL SOCIETY OF ARTS (RSA)

The RSA awards qualifications in office skills, including word-processing (now essential in many types of career), typing, accounting, computing, information technology and business studies. Some RSA qualifications can lead to certificates and NVQs. The courses are taken in schools, colleges, training centres and (normally for single subjects) at evening classes.

COURSES IN LAND-BASED INDUSTRIES

For information about courses, colleges and qualifications including NVQs, NEBAHAI (National Examinations Board for Agriculture, Horticulture and Allied Industries) National Certificates and Advanced National Certificates, BTEC National Diplomas and Higher National Diplomas and degrees, in subjects including farm management, countryside conservation and management, science and applied science (including food and food technology): *Directory of Courses in Land Based Industries* is available from Farming Press Books, Wharfedale Road, Ipswich IP1 4LG; 01473 241122.

The Agricultural Training Board – Landbase (ATB Landbase) and Warwickshire Careers Service publish a series of useful fact sheets which are available from ATB Landbase, NAC, Kenilworth, Warwickshire CV8 2LG.

TRAINING FOR WORK

Intended for people who have been unemployed for over 12 months, Training for Work is offered to people who wish to improve their work-related skills. Training is provided by your local Training and Enterprise Council and the type and amount of training available depends entirely on local requirements.

MODERN APPRENTICESHIPS

Designed for 16- and 17-year-old school-leavers, Modern Apprenticeships offer the apprentice training to at least NVQ level 3, which is roughly equivalent to two A levels or an Advanced GNVQ, and a small wage. Each apprenticeship lasts for about three years and the apprentice follows a training plan which is agreed at the start. By the end apprentices will have learned the skills needed to work in the chosen industry, and training also includes skills such as team work, communication and problem solving. About 40 different industries offer modern apprenticeships and those interested in finding out more should contact their local Jobcentre or careers office.

Accelerated Modern Apprenticeships
While very similar to the modern apprenticeship, the accelerated version is designed for 18- and 19-year-olds who may wish to build on skills and knowledge they already have. Again, there is a wage but this time the training programme takes between 18 months and two years only.

YOUTH TRAINING

Youth Training is designed to provide places for 16- and 17-year-old school-leavers with a programme of training and planned work experience, including off-the-job training or further education. Training vouchers may be available – so check with the Jobcentre. School-leavers of 16 are given two years of training including off-the-job training in a college or training centre; 17-year-olds have a one-year programme. Training can lead to NVQ, CGLI and RSA qualifications. The majority of places are work-based with employers. Many industries, such as hotel and catering, travel and tourism, hairdressing and other personal services recruit through YT schemes, as do large companies such as Unilever. Not all YT people are able to stay in permanent jobs at the end of the training period, but many do, and have a chance to prove themselves in non-academic ways. Details from Jobcentres or careers offices.

YOUTH CREDITS

Youth credits allow you to buy training. They are given to anyone who leaves school or college at 16 or 17, and their value can range from £750 to well over £5000, according to your particular needs and the occupational sector you choose. Credit is given in the form of a plastic card, cheque book or passport and may have a different local name, such as Training Credits. Once you have been given credit you can go out and spend it on the training you want, either Youth Training, a modern apprenticeship or one of the wide range of work-based training schemes available through TECs.

TIMING OF APPLICATIONS

Fifth year. If you have decided on the type of career that interests you, and would prefer to go to a college to take a vocational BTEC/SCOTVEC, CGLI or other course rather than staying on to do A levels at school, you will need to gather as much information about local colleges as you can, by attending any open days or evenings they hold, and by sending for prospectuses. There are also college courses in shorthand and typing, English, arithmetic, accounting data preparation, economics and law, leading to RSA (Royal Society of Arts) examinations; courses may be full time, part time during the day, or evening classes. Apply to companies for sponsorships between September and December.

Applications for courses normally need to be made during the spring term (by 31 January for Nursery Nursing Examination Board; otherwise by 31 March), and should be made as early as possible during the autumn term, especially for courses that are likely to prove popular. It is a good idea to apply for more than one course. Always double check the last date at which you can hand in your application form, and then make sure it is sent off well in advance of this date.

First year sixth. Short courses and open days will be organised by colleges and universities. Dates are listed in *Sixthformer's Guide*, published by the Independent Schools Careers Organisation (ISCO), 12a Princess Way, Camberley, Surrey GU15 3SP. The book may be available from school but if you want to order it the retail price is £3.95. Send for prospectuses and course details from March and April, although they may not all be available until the summer. Preliminary applications for Oxford and Cambridge first-choice colleges should be submitted during July.

Second year sixth. Applications for the Oxford conditional offer scheme must be in by mid-October (check date). Cambridge forms must also be in by mid-October. Oxbridge applicants' UCAS forms must be in by mid-October. Applications for other courses outside these schemes should be completed by early autumn. Other universities' and colleges' applications must be in by (and preferably earlier than) 15 December, including art foundation courses.

If you don't get your application in by then don't despair. It is still possible to be offered a place at a university and UCAS will accept applications until 30 June, although they will not be classified as priority but under consideration. Any applications submitted after this date will be put through a clearance process. It is still possible to be offered a place, even at this late stage, but the chances of getting the one you most wanted are greatly reduced.

Applications for sponsorship schemes should be made during the autumn term in many cases; the closing date is often 20 December. Other closing dates are at intervals until May; in some cases no date is specified, but early application is to be recommended (see next chapter). Applications for grants are made from January onwards.

During the autumn term, too, you should think about what you will do if you fail to get on to any of the courses you have applied for. If you think you would like to work for one of the large retailing firms, or for a bank or building society, or any other large organisation, you should apply to them during the autumn term; in many cases these organisations will be interviewing during the early part of the winter, or in February and March for summer entrants to their training schemes. Some banks recruit as early as November.

University and college decisions on applications on whether to make an unconditional offer, conditional offer (based on forthcoming examinations) or rejection are sent separately by UCAS and there is no need to reply to any offers until they have all been received. With the last decision, UCAS sends a statement of all decisions and the reply slip must be returned to UCAS within 14 days. Replies to offers must be received by UCAS not later than 15 May. Offers are confirmed by UCAS in mid-August to early September; remaining places are filled through Clearing throughout late August and September. Applicants for Art and Design courses can apply through two routes: Route A, or Route B – or through a combination of the two routes. In Route A, application forms should be submitted from the preceding September (initially, September 1996), and the normal UCAS deadline (15 December) and procedures apply. Decisions on these applications are due at the end of April, and replies to offers are required by the end of May. In Route B, application forms are submitted from January until the end of March and those applying are asked to express an interview preference – listing the colleges in order of preference. The UCAS *Handbook* identifies which courses recruit through Route A and which recruit through Route B. As there is a limit on the Route B list of only four colleges, candidates can use their remaining choices for Route A.

You should have heard by the beginning of May about all your university applications. Civil Service candidates should have applied for entry by 1 July. If you will be living away from home while studying you should make filling in your application for accommodation a priority.

IF YOU FAIL TO GET A COLLEGE PLACE

In the first instance, if a bad result is a genuine surprise both to your teachers and yourself, you can apply for a reassessment. Or you can retake the subject by staying on at school, by taking a course at an independent 'crammer' college, or it may be possible to take an intensive course at a further education college. In some cases, universities will not accept examination retakes, so this point must be checked. If you have failed all your A levels, you should think seriously about whether you are really academically up to a university course; it is possible that even if you passed the second time, you might find the course a struggle.

If you were successful enough to pass A levels, but with grades that were too low to be acceptable to your university choice, you should look at other college courses, and consider those, perhaps, with a more practical bias; a business studies course is a useful qualification. If you apply quickly you may get a place for the term that is about to start.

If you decide against further study, you can apply for training schemes with the Civil Service, financial institutions such as banks and insurance companies, or large organisations: they often prefer A level recruits to graduates on training schemes. While you are waiting to hear about your applications, it is a good idea to find yourself a job of some kind, where you are getting work experience, with the chance of staying on and progressing, should your other applications fail.

7. Can You Afford the Training?

The answer to the question above is, generally, 'Yes, if you are careful'. Even if you are careful there is a fair chance you will be in debt by the time you graduate. The days when students were entitled to housing benefit, income support and a grant large enough to cover the cost of living are long gone. Now students are expected to supplement their grant with a student loan, with many taking part-time jobs, either in the summer vacation or during term time.

GRANTS

The local education authority (LEA) pays the tuition fees and part of the maintenance costs of a student for full-time or sandwich courses and part-time initial teacher training courses leading to a first degree, the Diploma of Higher Education, BTEC Higher National Diploma awards, the Postgraduate Certificate in Education (PGCE) or the Art Teacher's Certificate or Diploma or a specified equivalent qualification.

Some teaching subjects are given a special status because they do not attract sufficient numbers of applicants. Science (chemistry, physics, biology), maths, design and technology, information technology, modern foreign languages (including Welsh) and religious education all attract funding. The bursary system has now been replaced by a more competitive tendering system whereby colleges and universities have to bid for funds from central government and decide for themselves how much to give students. This makes the whole situation very unclear and makes it impossible to say what the actual amount of additional money will be. The Teacher Training Agency communications centre at PO Box 3210, Chelmsford CM1 3WA (telephone 01245 454454) will be able to give you more up-to-the-minute news on this situation so it is worth contacting them.

There are some courses that are not eligible for 'mandatory' grants – that is, grants that the LEA *must* give. These are postgraduate studies, except postgraduate initial teacher training (but grants for these may be obtained from the relevant research council: Agricultural and Food, Medical, National Environment, Science and Engineering, or Social Science); courses that are part of the 'Articled Teachers Scheme'; nursing courses under the Project 2000 scheme; part-time courses – except some initial teacher training courses; non-degree courses for occupational therapists, orthoptists, physiotherapists which include remedial gymnasts, radiographers, dental hygienists or dental therapists (but contact the Department of Health, Student Grants Unit, Norcross, Blackpool FY5 3TA; 01253 856123 for information); courses of non-advanced further education such as GCSE and A levels, Scottish Highers, BTEC and SCOTVEC national awards (this does not include the Higher National Certificates or Diplomas); City and Guilds courses. The courses are normally taken in schools or on employers' training schemes, on a day-release or block-release basis and may be bought using Youth Credits. If this is not the case, or if staying on at school or attending a local college of further education is likely to cause hardship to parents, the LEA may award a 'discretionary' grant towards the cost of maintenance. Discretionary grants depend on how rich the LEA is feeling at the time – and LEAs are not known for feeling wealthy. So, while it is important to apply early for any grant, it is particularly vital in the case of discretionary grants.

There are certain stipulations about who can be eligible for both mandatory and discretionary grants; for instance, you should not have previously attended a course of advanced further education of more than two years (although one term's attendance will not matter). Full details about eligibility and other information about grants is given in *Student Grants and Loans: a brief guide*, from LEAs or from the Department for Education and Employment Publications Centre, PO Box 6927, London E13 3NZ.

Student Grants in Scotland is published by the Student Awards Agency for Scotland, Gyleview House, 3 Redheughs Rigg, South Gyle, Edinburgh EH12 9HH, and *Grants and Loans to Students* by the Department of Education for Northern Ireland, Rathgael House, Balloo Road, Bangor, County Down BT19 7PR. In addition, the Welsh Office Education Department publishes a Welsh language booklet on student grants and loans; FHE1 Division, 3rd Floor, Cathays Park, Cardiff CF1 3NQ.

The amounts of grant are lower than the 1990/91 level and have to be topped up with a student loan.

Grants

The level of grant each student receives is decided by the LEA, and is means-tested, based on parents' or spouse's income.

The basic grant rates are:

- Students living away from their parents' home and studying:
  in London: £2340
  elsewhere: £1885
- Students living at their parents' home: £1530

The LEA assesses the parents' income and works out whether they should contribute to the grant, and if so, how much. Contributions range from £45 for an income of £15,510 to £5800 for an income of £60,599 or more. If there are other dependent children the contribution is reduced.

There is an allowance for each extra week or part of a week of a course in the academic year above the basic limit of 30 weeks and three days (or, at Oxford or Cambridge, 25 weeks and three days). The amount of the grant also changes if a course includes a period of study abroad, and for students who are disabled.

LOANS

Government student loans are not means tested, but do have maximum limits, which change each year, and are administered by the Student Loans Company. The Company does not ask for a loan to begin being paid back until the April after the student finishes or leaves the course; the loans are paid back in a fixed number of monthly instalments, ideally over five years, and the amount is adjusted in line with inflation, but no interest is paid. In cases of low income (less than 85 per cent of average earnings) payments can be put off each year until you earn an amount laid down by the government, the 1995/96 threshold being £1267 per month.

For the year 1995/6 the maximum loan amount is:

- Students living away from their parents' home and studying:
  in London: Full year, £1695; final year, £1240
  elsewhere: Full year, £1385; final year, £1010
- Students living at their parents' home: Full year, £1065; final year, £780

A student living in hall could be spending around £50 per week on board and lodging – which includes heating, plenty of hot water, lighting and three meals a day. Renting a room (or house with other students) could be cheaper, but there are the electricity and gas bills to pay. A large chunk of the grant needs to be paid out in the first week at college, for lodgings and materials, such as books (which can be sold back secondhand to the students' union at the end of the course), and so it is important to apply for a grant early, so that it is ready for the start of the term.

After the initial spend, college budgeting can be managed by making use of the students' union bar, with free discos and live bands, and cheap entry to entertainments such as the college film society (maybe 80 films a year, for an outlay of only £20). The students who do manage on their grants and loans avoid the pubs! It is a good idea to keep a fail-safe sum in a building society to use in emergencies.

Students who get into serious financial difficulties can apply for help through the college from the Access Fund.

SPONSORSHIPS

Sponsorships are most readily available to students wanting to study subjects in which there is a need for a good supply of graduates – disciplines such as electronic and electrical engineering. The *Sponsorships for Students* book published by Biblios (see page 98) gives details of firms willing to sponsor students. There is also *Engineering Opportunities* (see page 98). You need to apply early for sponsorship; there could be 2500 hopefuls chasing only 50 places.

An advantage of sponsorship is that you have a guaranteed place for work experience on a sandwich course – and there is the possibility of a job with the sponsor at the end of your training.

Other publications that you may find helpful are: *Charities Digest*, published by the Family Welfare Association; *Directory of Grant-making Trusts*, published by the Charities Aid Foundation and *The Grant Register*, published by Macmillan. Some of these books are expensive, so ask in your local library.

Part 4

8. Where to Go for Further Careers Advice

Industrialists, someone at the Institute of Management told me, are the world's worst communicators – they are good at getting on and doing the job themselves, but not at telling people what they are doing. However, they are attempting to change that by taking sixth formers and young people from school to try to give them a taste of the working environment; so it is worth taking advantage of any visits or lectures about the world of work, just to get a better picture of the opportunities available, even if it is connected with some activity that doesn't immediately appeal to you.

This principle also applies to colleges and universities; you will learn far more about the atmosphere of student life if you take part in visits arranged by the school, or listen to talks given by local college lecturers at school. When you visit colleges, including any visit you make for an interview, talk as much as possible to students who are already there to find out what they think of it, and what life there is like.

You can do more research within your school careers library and the local library. There will be books of a general nature, and others specifically about different careers. Look for *Occupations*, updated by COIC every year, which covers a wide range of careers and jobs, and the qualifications needed for them. Careers libraries cannot afford to stock every relevant book published, but your careers teacher or local careers officer will be able to tell you where you can find out more.

There are careers libraries and careers service staff in universities and colleges, too. They also hold 'summer recruitment fairs' at which employers interview and recruit students in their last year at college as part of what the employers quaintly call the 'milk round'. (The milk rounds take place in the spring and summer.)

Approaching the subject of choosing a career from another angle, careers officers (and commercial careers agencies) use computer-backed systems for finding out students' aptitudes and interests, and matching them up with suitable areas of work.

They aim to identify the broad areas first, then to provide ideas on the relevant jobs within these areas that could be explored as possible careers, and finally to supply information about each job – a brief description of what it involves, details of skills and/or qualifications needed. This system is available in many schools as part of a careers education programme. You can use it to give yourself pointers towards careers which you can then find out more about – the COIC Signposts box, which will be in your school careers library, will help here. It flags up job titles in the areas which interest you and follows this up with more specific information about what the work actually entails, focusing on four or five different jobs in detail. Remember, though, that while there will be plenty of information from long-established employers, such as the police and the armed services, there will be less from the industrial side, where everyone may be too busy designing robots or selling pharmaceuticals to developing countries to have time to devote to providing careers information.

However, writing to the schools liaison officers or personnel offices of the large companies, such as GEC-Marconi or ICI, and to professional organisations, such as the British Medical Association, will elicit useful careers information and interesting literature.

There are also independent vocational guidance agencies, such as Career Analysts, 90 Gloucester Place, London W1H 4BL, who charge a fee (not small) to give individual guidance. The Independent Schools Careers Organisation (ISCO), 12a Princess Way, Camberley, Surrey GU15 3SP, runs courses and conferences as part of a careers guidance scheme, and a useful ISCO Careers Bulletin covers various aspects of careers information.

Finally, you will find that individuals, either those you know personally, or those you contact for information, will be very keen to give both help and advice.

9. Useful Addresses

If you have found an area of work that particularly interests you write to one of the following organisations for more information. They publish material of varying length and price so when you make your first enquiry it might be useful to enclose a stamped, self-addressed envelope. Always ask for a publications leaflet and for any free careers literature which they may produce.

The Arts Council, 14 Great Peter Street, London SW1P 3NQ; 0171 333 0100

Association of British Pharmaceutical Industries (ABPI), 12 Whitehall, London SW1A 2DY; 0171 930 3477 (for graduate careers booklet)

Association of Graduate Careers Advisory Service (AGCAS), Central Services Unit, Armstrong House, Oxford Road, Manchester M1 7ED; 0161 236 9816 (acts on behalf of graduate careers advisory services; provides publications and services)

Banking Information Service, 10 Lombard Street, London EC3V 9AT; 0171 626 9386

The BioIndustry Association, 14–15 Belgrave Square, London SW7 2DZ; 0171 245 9911

British Computer Society, 1 Stanford Street, Swindon SN1 1HJ; 01793 417417

British Medical Association, BMA House, Tavistock Square, London WC1H 9JP; 0171 387 4499

British Polymer Training Association, Coppice House, Halesfield 7, Telford, Shropshire TF7 4NA; 01952 587020

Business and Technology Education Council (BTEC), Central House, Upper Woburn Place, London WC1H 0HH; 0171 413 8400 (for information on BTEC courses)

Business in the Community, 8 Stratton Street, London W1X 5FD; 0171 629 1600

Career Analysts, 90 Gloucester Place, London W1H 4BL; 0171 935 5452

Careers and Occupational Information Centre (COIC), Moorfoot, Sheffield S1 4PQ; 0114 275 3275

Careers Research and Advisory Centre (CRAC), Sheraton House, Castle Park, Cambridge CB3 0AX; 01223 460277

Central Bureau for Educational Visits and Exchanges, 10 Spring Gardens, London SW1A 2BN; 0171 389 4004

Central Services Unit, Armstrong House, Oxford Road, Manchester M1 7ED; 0161 236 9816 (for information on graduate careers and appointments)

The Chartered Association of Certified Accountants, 29 Lincoln's Inn Fields, London WC2A 3EE; 0171 396 5800

Chartered Insurance Institute, 20 Aldermanbury, London EC2V 7HY; 0171 606 3835

City and Guilds, 1 Giltspur Street, London EC1A 9DD; 0171 294 2468

Civil Engineering Careers Service, 1–7 Great George Street, London SW1P 3AA; 0171 222 7722

College of Occupational Therapists, Education Department, 6–8 Marshalsea Road, London SE1 1TY; 0171 357 6480

College of Speech and Language Therapists, 7 Bath Place, Rivington Street, London EC2A 1XX; 0171 613 3855

Committee of Vice-Chancellors and Principals of the Universities of the United Kingdom, 29 Tavistock Square, London WC1H 9EZ; 0171 387 9231

Communications, Advertising and Marketing Education Foundation, Abford House, 15 Wilton Road, London SW1X 8QS; 0171 828 7506

Computing Services and Software Association, 5th Floor, Hanover House, 73–74 High Holborn, London WC1V 6LE; 0171 405 2171

Construction Industry Training Board, Bircham Newton, King's Lynn, Norfolk PE21 6RH; 01553 776677 (ext 2466)

Council for Professions Supplementary to Medicine, Park House, 184 Kennington Park Road, London SE11 4BU; 0171 582 0866

Council of Legal Education, Inns of Court School of Law, 39 Eagle Street, London WC1R 4AJ; 0171 404 5787

Department for Education and Employment, Sanctuary Buildings, Great Smith Street, Westminster, London SW1P 3BT; 0171 925 5000

Department of Health, Health Service Careers, Richmond House, 79 Whitehall, London SW1A 2NS; 0171 210 3000

Department of Trade and Industry, 1 Victoria Street, London SW1H 0ET; 0171 215 5000

Engineering Careers Information Service, 41 Clarendon Road, Watford, Hertfordshire WD1 1HS; 01923 238411

Engineering Council, 10 Maltravers Street, London WC2R 3ER; 0171 240 7891

General Dental Council, 37 Wimpole Street, London W1M 8QD; 0171 486 2171

Hotel and Catering Training Company, Careers Information Service, International House, High Street, London W5 5DB; 0181 579 2400

Hotel Catering and International Management Association, 191 Trinity Road, London SW17 7HN; 0181 672 4251

Independent Schools Careers Organisation, 12a–18a Princess Way, Camberley, Surrey GU15 3SP; 01276 21188

Institute of Chartered Accountants in England and Wales, PO Box 433, Moorgate Place, London EC2P 2BJ; 0171 920 8100

The Institute of Chartered Accountants of Scotland, 27 Queen Street, Edinburgh EH2 1LA; 0131 225 5673

Institute of Legal Executives, Kempston Manor, Kempston, Bedford MK42 7AB; 01234 841000

Institute of Leisure and Amenity Management, ILAM House, Lower Basildon, Reading, Berkshire RG8 9NE; 01491 874222

Institute of Linguists, 24a Highbury Grove, London N5 2DQ; 0171 359 7445

Institute of Management, Management House, Cottingham Road, Corby, Northamptonshire NN17 1TT; 01536 204222

Institute of Personnel Development, IPD House, Camp Road, Wimbledon, London SW19 4UX; 0181 946 9100

Institute of Medical Laboratory Sciences, 12 Coldbath Square, London EC1R 5HL; 0171 636 8192

The Institution of Chemical Engineers, Davis Building, 165–189 Railway Terrace, Rugby CV21 3HQ; 01788 578214

The Institution of Electrical Engineers, Schools Education and Liaison, Michael Faraday House, Six Hills Way, Stevenage, Hertfordshire SG1 2AY; 0171 240 1871

The Institution of Mechanical Engineers, 1 Birdcage Walk, London SW1H 9JH; 0171 222 7899 (for *Sponsorship and Training Opportunities in Engineering*)

119

The Law Society, Careers and Recruitment Service, 227–228 Strand, London WC2R 1BA; 0171 242 1222

Local Government Management Board, Arndale House, Arndale Centre, Luton, Bedfordshire LU1 2TS; 01582 451166

National Association of Teachers in Higher Education, Hamilton House, Mabledon Place, London WC1H 9BJ; 0171 387 1441

National Council for the Training of Journalists, Latton Bush Centre, Southern Way, Harlow, Essex CM18 7BL; 01279 430009

NCVQ, 222 Euston Road, London NW1 2BZ; 0171 387 9898

Office of Public Servants, Graduates and School Liaison, Room 127/2, The Cabinet Office, Horse Guards Road, London SW1P 3AL

Police Careers, Room 516, Home Office, Queen Anne's Gate, London SW1H 9AT

Police Division, Scottish Home and Health Department, St Andrews House, Edinburgh EH1 3DE

RASE (Royal Agricultural Society of England)/Warwickshire Careers Service, 10 Northgate Street, Warwick CV34 4SR; 01926 410410

Recruitment and Assessment Services (Civil Service), Alençon Link, Basingstoke, Hampshire RG21 1JB; 01256 29222

Royal Institute of British Architects (RIBA), 66 Portland Place, London W1N 4AD; 0171 580 5533

The Royal Institution of Chartered Surveyors, Education and Training Department, Surveyor Court, Westwood Way, Coventry CV4 8JE; 0171 222 7000 or 01203 694757

RSA Examinations Board, Westwood Way, Coventry CV4 8HS; 01203 470033

Scottish Education Department, 43 Jeffrey Street, Edinburgh EH1 1DN; 0131 556 8400

Scottish Enterprise Foundation, University of Stirling, Stirling FK9 4LA; 01786 473171

Scottish Vocational Education Council (SCOTVEC), Hanover House, 24 Douglas Street, Glasgow G2 7NQ; 0141 248 7900

Skill, the National Bureau for Students with Disabilities, 336 Brixton Road, London SW9 7AA; 0171 274 0565

Society of Surveying Technicians, Surveyor Court, Westwood Way, Coventry CV4 8JE

SPRIG Sport and Recreation Information Group, Sports Council, 16 Upper Woburn Place, London WC1H 0QP; 0171 388 1277

Student Awards Agency for Scotland, Gyleview House, 3 Redheughs Rigg, South Gyle, Edinburgh EH12 9HH

Teacher Training Agency, Information Section, Portland House, Stag Place, London SW1E 5TT; 0171 925 3700
TEC, Employment Department, Moorfoot, Sheffield S1 4PQ; 0114 275 3275

Universities and Colleges Admissions Service (UCAS), Fulton House, Jessop Avenue, Cheltenham, Gloucestershire GL50 3SA; 01242 222444

Women in Banking and Finance, 55 Bourne Vale, Hayes, Bromley, Kent BR2 7NW
Women into Computing, Open University, 4 Portwall Lane, Bristol BS1 6ND; 0117 929 9641
Women in Management, 64 Marryat Road, Wimbledon, London SW19 5BN (moving soon)
Women in the Public Sector Network, Touche Ross, No 1 Stone Cutter Street, Stone Cutter Square, London EC4; 0171 936 3000

10. *Further Reading*

The following titles are published by Kogan Page:

British Qualifications (annual)
Great Answers to Tough Interview Questions: How to Get the Job You Want (3rd edition), Martin John Yate
How to Pass A Levels and GNVQs (3rd edition), Howard Barlow
How to Pass Graduate Recruitment Tests, Mike Bryon
How to Pass Numeracy Tests, Harry Tolley and Ken Thomas
How to Pass Selection Tests, Mike Bryon and Sanjay Modha
How to Pass Technical Selection Tests, Mike Bryon and Sanjay Modha
How to Pass the Civil Service Qualifying Tests, Mike Bryon
How to Pass Verbal Reasoning Tests, Harry Tolley and Ken Thomas
How You Can Get That Job!: Application Forms and Letters Made Easy, Rebecca Corfield
How to Win as a Part-Time Student, Tom Bourner and Phil Race
Interviews Made Easy, Mark Parkinson
The Job Hunter's Handbook, David Greenwood
Job Hunting Made Easy (3rd edition), John Bramham and David Cox
Making it in Sales: A Career Guide for Women, Mary J Foster with Timothy R V Foster
Manage Your Own Career, Ben Bell
Preparing Your Own CV, Rebecca Corfield
Readymade Job Search Letters, Lynn Williams
Test Your Own Aptitude (2nd edition), Jim Barrett and Geoff Williams
Working Abroad: The Daily Telegraph Guide to Working and Living Overseas (18th edition), Godfrey Golzen
Working for Yourself: The Daily Telegraph Guide to Self-Employment (16th edition), Godfrey Golzen
Your First Job (2nd edition), Vivien Donald and Ray Grose

Index

Universities and Colleges
Admissions Service 99, 100, 106
University courses 95–101

Valuation, *see* Surveying
Veterinary surgeon 31, 35, 39, 56,
66, 67, 71, 73, 75, 81, 95
Voluntary Service Overseas 71, 81

Women at work 87–91; in armed
services 34; in computing 13; in
engineering 74; in law 47, 48; self-
employment 61

Working abroad 69–72
Working alone 81
Writer 25

Youth Training (YT) 104

Zoology 56, 96